HITLER'S WAR MACHINE

POLAND 1939
THE BLITZKRIEG UNLEASHED

BY BOB CARRUTHERS

Pen & Sword
MILITARY

This edition published in 2013 by
Pen & Sword Military
An imprint of
Pen & Sword Books Ltd
47 Church Street
Barnsley
South Yorkshire
S70 2AS

First published in Great Britain in 2011 in digital format by
Coda Books Ltd.

Copyright © Coda Books Ltd, 2011
Published under licence by Pen & Sword Books Ltd.

ISBN 978 1 78159 227 4

A CIP catalogue record for this book is
available from the British Library

Printed and bound in Great Britain by
CPI Group (UK) Ltd, Croydon, CR0 4YY

Pen & Sword Books Ltd incorporates the Imprints of Pen & Sword Aviation, Pen & Sword Family
History, Pen & Sword Maritime, Pen & Sword Military, Pen & Sword Discovery, Pen & Sword
Politics, Pen & Sword Atlas, Pen & Sword Archaeology, Wharncliffe Local History, Wharncliffe
True Crime, Wharncliffe Transport, Pen & Sword Select, Pen & Sword Military Classics, Leo
Cooper, The Praetorian Press, Claymore Press, Remember When, Seaforth Publishing and Frontline
Publishing

For a complete list of Pen & Sword titles please contact
PEN & SWORD BOOKS LIMITED
47 Church Street, Barnsley, South Yorkshire, S70 2AS, England
E-mail: enquiries@pen-and-sword.co.uk
Website: www.pen-and-sword.co.uk

CONTENTS

CHAPTER 1

The Re-birth of Poland

T he reborn Polish state, which was formed in November 1918, emerged into life in the most difficult circumstances imaginable. The entire country presented a depressing picture of ruin and poverty. Polish territory had been the scene of heavy fighting between the Central Powers and the Russians in the opening stages of World War I. In addition the German and Austrian occupation forces had systematically exploited the country in the several years that followed and stripped Poland of much of her economic capacity. The end of the Great War found Poland's factories destroyed or idle, its livestock decimated, and the nation's economy in a state of chaos. For Poland however there was to be no immediate chance to rebuild. There was no safe respite from the spectre of war.

The almost immediate onset of war against, first Soviet Ukraine then Soviet Russia over disputed territory in the Ukraine further plagued the young nation between 1919 and 1920. Polish forces were at one point pressed right back to the gates of Warsaw before seizing the initiative to drive the Soviets right back to their own borders.

All of this did further damage to the fragile economic life of Poland and to add further hardship to this unhappy mix there was also a period Fierce fighting against the ethnic German self defence forces in Upper Silesia (The Selbstchutz Oberschleisen). The Selbstchutz Oberschleisen soon received illicit reinforcement in the form of the German paramilitary Freikorps and fierce fighting raged in Poland's Upper Silesian territory throughout May, June and July 1921 at one point in July 1921 the situation got so bad that a complete withdrawal of Polish armed forces from the region had to be under taken.

Eventually a peace was established on both fronts The Peace Of Riga signed on 18th March 1921 concluded peace with the Soviets and in August 1921 the Freikorps were disbanded under political pressure. Finally in late 1921 the process of reconstruction and economic recovery was at

"To Arms - save our homeland!" A Polish propaganda poster from the Polish-Soviet war

Polish troops man a machine gun position during the war with Soviet Russia, which raged between 1919 and 1921.

last begun. All of this turmoil of course meant that Poland started the recovery process three years later than elsewhere and would therefore lag behind other World War I participants in the process of modernisation and recovery.

However the Poles are an industrious people and despite these disadvantages Poland made considerable progress in the short period of its existence as a peaceful modern state. By 1939 the Polish State in 1939 was established as a republic, organized under the new, and nominally democratic, constitution of 23rd April 1935. The President was chosen indirectly by an assembly of electors, who were themselves elected by popular vote. The legislature consisted of a senate and Sejm, or lower house. Elections to the legislature were held every five years except for one-third of the senate seats, filled by Presidential appointment.

The President served for a term of seven years, and nominated his own ministers. As Chief of State, the President controlled the usual executive organs of government. In practice, the Polish President was a strong figure, mainly due to the influence of Marshal Pilsudski, who was the power behind the government almost continuously from the time of its founding until the new constitution was written and put into force a month before his death on 12th May 1935.

Ignace Moscicki, a close personal friend of Pilsudski, served as President in 1939. Jozef Beck was Foreign Minister and Marshal Edward Rydz-Smigly was the Inspector General of the Armed Forces. These three and a few others controlled what was essentially an authoritarian form of government, wherein the executive branch of the government dominated the legislature. Despite their own National Socialist form of dictatorship, the Germans took full advantage of the opportunity to criticize the Polish government of representing its own form of authoritarianism in the highly effective propaganda campaign run by Josef Goebels.

Population and economy

As of the beginning of 1939 the Polish State had a total population of 35 million, of whom 22 million were ethnic Poles. The larger minorities were the Ukrainians amounting to three million, Jews also numbering in the region of 3 million, Ruthenians amounting to two million, and the ethnic Germans who numbered 750,000. Smaller numbers of Russians, Lithuanians, Slovaks, and other Slavic groups comprised the remainder of the minorities resident within Poland's borders.

Sixty five percent of this population was engaged in agriculture, producing large quantities of grain, potatoes, sugar beet, and dairy products for export. With 23 percent of its area covered by forests, chiefly in the east and Carpathian Mountains regions, lumber was also an important item for export. Some coal was also shipped abroad, from the mining region southwest of Cracow.

Poland's mineral deposits included substantial reserves of coal, lignite (brown coal), oil, potassium salts (important in the manufacture of gunpowder and fertilizers), and zinc. Poland produced approximately 2 million tons of steel yearly, 40 million tons of coal, and half a million tons of petroleum products.

Poland's chief export customer as well as the source of most of Poland's imports was Germany. In exchange for foodstuffs and lumber, Germany shipped to Poland large numbers of motor vehicles and machines, as well as textiles, finished metal goods, and chemicals. A favourable rate of exchange for the German mark prompted many Germans in the border areas to buy leather goods and other consumer products in Poland. The low wage level of its workers gave Poland some advantage in competing in the world's markets.

The Polish merchant marine in 1939, according to Lloyd's Register, comprised 63 vessels and 121,630 gross tons. Poland's sole port, Gdynia, had been rapidly built into a center of commerce from the small fishing village which had existed in 1919, and Poland had free access to the excellent facilities of the harbour at Danzig.

The terrain

Within Poland itself, there were over 3,800 miles of navigable rivers and canals, including 1,534 miles of the Vistula. These supplemented the 12,000 miles of government-operated railway lines for moving heavy freight. Poland also possessed 37,000 miles of improved highways. Commercial air transportation was not significant by western European standards.

Poland forms a vast land bridge from the North German Plain in the west to the marshy lowlands of Belorussia (White Russia) and the rich steppe of the Ukraine in the east. The country possesses no good natural defence lines, except to a limited degree in the Carpathian Mountains in the south, and along the course of the Narew, Vistula, and San Rivers, which bisect Poland in a general north-south line. Operations by any but very small infantry forces would be almost impossible in the vast Pripyat Marshes in the east. As of August 1939 the area of Poland comprised 150,470 square miles, a landmass slightly smaller in extent than the American state of California.

Along the southern frontier, the Carpathian Mountains reach their greatest altitude in the High Tatra, with peaks up to 8,700 feet. The passes through the mountains are limited in number, but the most difficult areas to traverse lie on the Czech side and several roads and rail lines give direct access to the industrial region in southwestern Poland. However, infantry, preferably mountain infantry, would still be necessary to force many of the passes into Poland if they were defended.

North of the mountains, the Carpathian Plain merges into the southern upland area of Poland, which extends from Cracow in a northeasterly direction to Lublin and includes the rich plateau of Galicia. The uplands reach altitudes of 2,000 feet in some places, though their average elevation is much less. The area is gene-rally well suited to the conduct of military operations by motorised and armoured units as well as by infantry.

North of this upland region is the extensive Central Polish Plain, extending from Poznan to Warsaw and the east, and merging into the Pripyat Marshes, which continue into White Russia. The Central Plain is the largest area of the country and has come to be regarded as typical of Poland's geography; it has long been the center of Polish national life. The terrain and the road and rail network of this area offer excellent opportunities for military operations, in particular the use of armour.

To the north of the Central Polish Plain is another belt of uplands extending from German Pomerania to East Prussia, Lithuania, and White Russia. These uplands on Poland's northern border reach elevations of 600-700 feet, but form no natural boundary with East Prussia. In the Polish Corridor, the low hills west of the Polish port of Gdynia form little obstacle to north-south or east-west movement.

The climate of Poland becomes increasingly continental from west to east, with correspondingly wider ranges in daily and annual temperatures. In the more easterly regions of the country, summers are quite warm and the winter season cold, with heavy snowfall. Poland generally has abundant rain, causing frequent flooding of the rivers in the more level portions of the country. These floods could form a serious obstacle to the conduct of extensive military operations.

The chief river is the Vistula, which rises just inside the Polish frontier southwest of Cracow, wends its way through the west central part of Poland, bisects the capital, Warsaw, and empties into the sea at Danzig. Other major rivers of Central Poland are the Bug, San, and Narew, all of which flow into the Vistula. In the west, the Warta (Wartha) flows into Germany and becomes a tributary of the Oder. In the southeast the Dniester flows into Romania and the Soviet Union. In the east central portion of Poland a number of smaller rivers flow into the Pripyat Marshes. In the northeast the Niemen flows from east to west across that extension of Poland bordered by White Russia and Lithuania, to flow into the latter country, and the Dzisna flows across the frontier to the east to become the Soviet Union's Dvina. With their bridges destroyed, all of these rivers could form obstacles to the movement of troops, particularly armoured and motorized units. With the rivers in flood, the

The command contingent form a Polish cavalry regiment taken in 1920 during the course of the war with Soviet Russia.

obstacles in some places would be all but insurmountable.

As expected The weather remained warm and dry in late August 1939, with no immediate prospect of the heavy rains that would cause the rivers to flood and turn the countryside into a muddy morass. Instead, the Polish plains offered excellent opportunities to German military operations, and the movement of armoured and motorized units. Poland's terrain was well suited for mobile operations when the weather cooperated. Poland has extensive flat plains with long frontiers totalling almost 5,600 kilometers (3,500 miles), Poland's long border with Germany on the west and north (facing East Prussia) extended to some 2,000 kilometers (1,250 miles). Those frontiers had been lengthened by another 300 kilometers (180 miles) on the southern side in the aftermath of the Munich Agreement of 1938; the German incorporation of Bohemia and Moravia and creation of the German puppet state of Slovakia meant that Poland's new southern flank was exposed to Hitler's ambitions. The problems posed by the extended frontiers were to prove insurmountable for the Poles and German planners intended to fully exploit their huge border with the great enveloping manoeuvre envisaged under the Fall Weiss plan under German units were to invade Poland from three directions. From within Poland, the German minority would assist by engaging in diversion and sabotage operations through Selbstschutz Oberschleisen (Self Defence) units, which had been active since 1921 long before Hitler's war was envisaged.

CHAPTER 2

The Road to War

A Polish state had not existed since the Congress of Vienna in1814 and in 1918 the exact boundaries of the new republic's territory had therefore to be defined once more. This took a great deal of political juggling and led to outright military conflict in the form of the Polish Soviet war of 1919-1921. As we have seen that war was concluded by the Peace of Riga which set the eastern boundaries of Poland during the inter war years. The Poles had been in the ascendant when the peace was declared and the extra territory extracted from the Soviets was to remain a bone of contention until 1945.

Danzig and the Corridor

The tensions in the east were mirrored in the west. The territorial clauses of the treaty of Versailles between Germany and the Allies allowed for the creation of the Corridor a strip of territory taken from Germany which was designed to create an area of territory linking Poland to the Baltic.

Poland had previously enjoyed such a land corridor in the 1770s and giving the reborn Poland access to the sea was one of the guarantees proposed by the United States President Woodrow Wilson in his famous Fourteen Points of 1918. The thirteenth of Wilson's points was: "An independent Polish state should be erected which should include the territories inhabited by indisputably Polish populations, which should be assured a free and secure access to the sea, and whose political and economic independence and territorial integrity should be guaranteed by international covenant."

This was certainly a controversial measure. It was designed to provide Poland with unfettered access to the Baltic Sea by means of an area of land, which led north to the site of the port of Gdnyia. The city of Danzig, now better known by its modern name of Gdansk, was a free state and not included in the corridor. This strip of land had been appropriated at the expense of German territory and soon became known simply as the Corridor. It was viewed by many as an artificial device and this highly unsatisfactory arrangement had a further disadvantage in that it isolated the province of East Prussia from Germany, disrupted much of the Reich's economy, and placed thousands of Germans living in The Corridor within the borders of the new Polish state. Worse still East Prussia was totally cut off from the rest of the Reich and this festering sore was to ultimately lead to the conflagration of World War II. Recognising the difficulties posed for Danzig the major a major port at the mouth of the Vistula and populated almost completely by Germans, was made a free city. It was furnished with a League of Nations commissioner and its own elected legislature.

Poland however was permitted to control Danzig's customs, to represent the Free City in foreign affairs, and to keep a small military force in the harbour area where they were housed in a small fort known as The Westerplatte. A plebiscite was held to determine the frontier in parts of Upper Silesia and the population voted in favour of Germany, but the Poles moved quickly and secured several of the more desirable areas by force by a sudden military action which began on 18th August 1919. A Polish-French treaty of alliance signed on 19th February 1921 was designed to maintain these territorial arrangements and cement these new boundaries in place. The quid pro quo as far as the French were concerned was that the existence of a major new ally served to provide France with an eastern counterweight to the threat of future German expansion.

There were historical ethnic, economic and political arguments in favour of the creation of the Corridor of these the ethnic situation was the most obviously justifiable reason for returning the area to the new Polish state. A Polish corridor had existed in 1772, which had been extinguished by a combination of the rise of Prussian military might and Russian expansionism. Nonetheless the majority of the population in the area was still Polish. The Polish commission report to the Allied Supreme Council was made on 12th March 1919 and it made clear the case for the creation of the Corridor on ethnic grounds. "Finally the fact must be recognised that 600,000 Poles in West Prussia would under any alternative plan remain under German rule".

The Prussian census of 1910 also supported the ethnic case. It revealed that there were 528,000 Poles, including a substantial number of West Slavic Kashubians, who had supported the Polish national lists in German elections in the region. These numbers compared strongly against just 385,000 Germans even if one included German troops stationed in the area. The Poles naturally did not want the Polish population to remain under the control of the German state, which had in the recent past treated the Polish population and other minorities as second-class citizens and pursued an unwelcome policy of "Germanisation" against the minorities within the boundaries of the greater German Reich. Polish-born Professor Lewis Bernstein Namier was among those who advocated the creation of the Corridor despite the fact that the population in the costal areas was overwhelmingly German. He wrote a lengthy article for the Manchester Guardian on November 7th, 1933 in which he strongly stated his case for the Corridor to be controlled by Poland. "The Poles are the Nation of the Vistula, and their settlements extend from the sources of the river to its estuary.... It is only fair that the claim of the river-basin should prevail against that of the seaboard."

The Upper Silesian crisis of 1921

The treatment of ethnic Germans living in Silesia was harsh. The forces of law and order in the new Polish state, it appeared to many ethnic Germans, turned a blind eye to the widespread brutalities which occurred as old scores were settled and a new order introduced. This unhappy situation eventually resulted in the 1921 crisis in Upper Silesia. The hastily formed Selbschtuz Oberschleisen took the field against the regular Polish army and managed to hold their own in the early fighting.

Fettered by the treaty of Versailles, the Reichsheer (the regular German army) could not

Marshal Pilsudski the father of the reborn Polish state. Marshal Pilsudski was the real power behind the government until his death on 12th May 1935.

act in support of the ethnic Germans, but one possible solution did present itself in the form of the Freikorps. These nationalist paramilitary units were drawn from the ranks of battle hardened world war one veterans. They had successfully countered the communists in Germany were pledged to defending the interests of the Greater German Reich as they interpreted those interests. Three battalions of these tough auxiliaries in the form of the Oberland Freikorps were sent to the aid of the local Selbstschutz Oberscleisen, which were still engaged in fighting the Polish regular army. The very existence of the Freikorps, which was clearly as an auxiliary military force, was highly questionable under the terms of the Versailles treaty and unwelcome questions were immediately raised by the Allies. Oblivious to the political machinations the Freikorps got on with the job in hand. These were ideologically motivated warriors who were hard nosed veterans of the Great War. Their whole raison d'etre was to fight in the cause of German interests and honour . A notable victory was gained by these irregular but highly effective troop over Polish regular forces at Annaberg in May 1921. As the shock news of the Polish defeat spread political pressure mounted and the first inklings of that pressure came in the form of a threat from France that they would withdraw their peace keeping forces from Silesia, leaving the ethnic Germans totally at the mercy of the Poles. Despite the effectiveness of their military contribution the political tide in Germany soon began to run against the activities of the Freikorps in Poland who were dismissed as "gangs of thugs". Nonetheless the Freikorps continued to fight on. Further victories in the field around Ratisbon eventually forced the Poles to bow to British pressure evacuate Upper Silesia on 5th July 1921.

These gains were to prove in vain however. The obvious breach of the Versailles treaty was to great to ignore and this eventually forced the embarrassed Weimar Republic to order the withdrawal and disbandment of the Freikorps. This order was obeyed after a fashion although many weapons were buried rather than surrendered and a large portion of the Freikorps remained behind in Upper Silesia where, in anticipation of further trouble, they worked under cover posing as agricultural labourers and forestry workers. Despite heated German protests, which received strong British support for Germany over what was obviously a reciprocal Polish breach of the terms of The Treaty Of Versailles, the areas seized by the Poles by force from Germany were nevertheless incorporated into Poland.

On returning to Germany The Freikorps veterans loudly proclaimed that they had been "stabbed in the back " by the representatives of a state whose interests they had sought to protect. As these Great War veterans already considered themselves to have been betrayed once before, the wounds were beginning to run deep. An embittered sense of alienation and an overriding desire for revenge fuelled their nationalist ambitions, which centred around a crusade to restore the lost honour and power of the Reich. Among the ranks of the departing Freikorps was the notorious Sepp Dietrich. From the evidence of the fact that he was awarded the Silesian eagle First Class, a decoration which was only presented to veterans in recognition of six months field service in Silesia, it appears that Dietrich was one of those who remained behind in anticipation of further flare ups. He seems to have slipped back into Germany in October 1921 some three months after the disbandment of the Freikorps. Dietrich was one on many Freikorps veterans who felt he had a score to settle and he would return to Poland seventeen years later in more sinister form as a battalion commander in the ranks of the SS Verfüngungstruppe (SS Special Purpose Troops), the forerunners of the fearsome Waffen SS.

Germany, of course, was still the defeated pariah after world war one and in the twenties

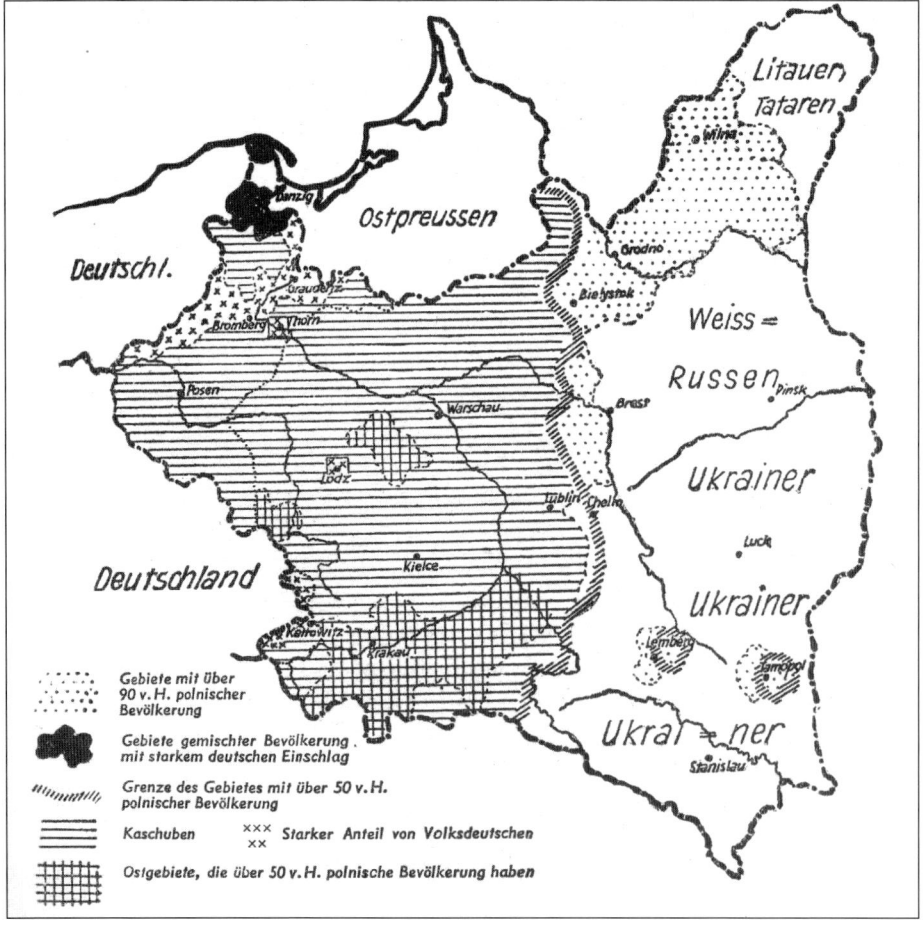

The population distribution in Poland from a contemporary German publication. The ethnic German population was concentrated in the North East of the country.

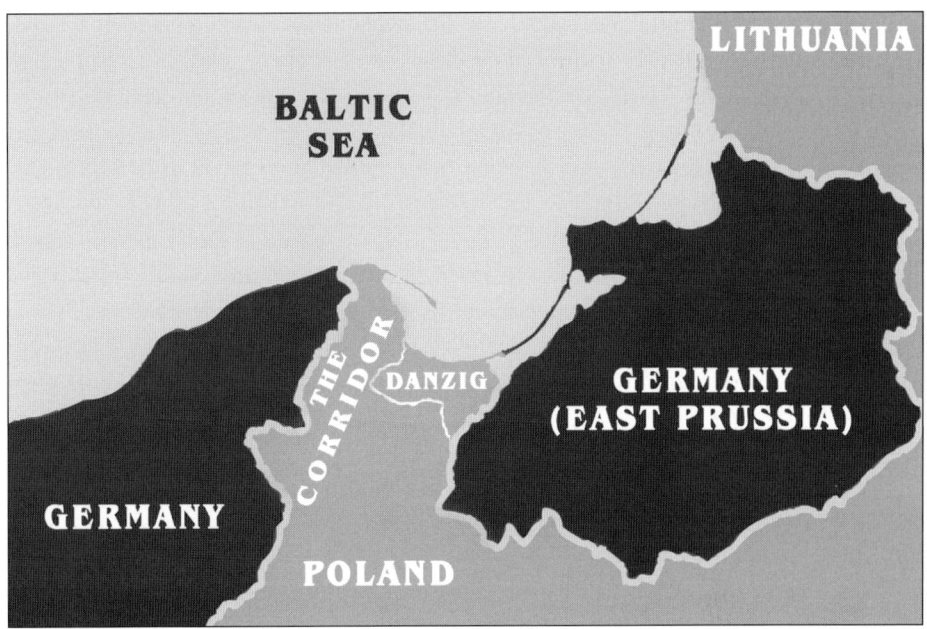

The tensions over the Polish corridor were to lead directly to World War II.

and had other more substantial concerns than honour or glory. She was rightly preoccupied with her own massive internal troubles. Germany had been reduced to the position of an inferior power and in the years that followed there were troubles aplenty. In the early twenties The Reich was beset with hyperinflation and plagued by massive unemployment. The Nationalist focus on ephemeral issues such as national prestige ranked low by comparison, but there were many who felt strongly about nationalist issues and slowly they would begin to coalesce around a peculiar young war veteran called Adolf Hitler.

Hitler assumes power

After twelve years of political struggle In 1933 Adolf Hitler finally became chancellor. He brought with him what was hailed as a new and revolutionary system of government to the Reich. Hitler's political ambitions had been made clear in his infamous semi-autobiographical "Mein Kampf". Hitler outlined the importance of propaganda. This powerful new device in the sinister hands of Goebels reached a new and unprecedented level. The National Socialist regime quickly assumed complete control over Germany's national life and future in a manner, which was completely unheralded. . backed by a relentless stream of propaganda nationalist issues now assumed pre-eminence. One of Hitler's first measures was to introduce an extensive armaments program, the rapid expansion of the armed forces, and public construction work. Together these measures brought Germany a measure of economic recovery and certainly improved the country's military position. Under Hitler events moved swiftly Germany soon regained a semblance of the ascendancy it had held as a European power before her defeat in 1918.

Hitler of course was another of the many veterans who believed that Germany had not in fact been defeated in World War I at all. He subscribed to the widely held view that her armed forces had been stabbed in the back by the actions ungrateful politicians, communists and Jews. For Hitler the Versailles treaty was the biggest betrayal of all it haunted his twisted psyche. He desired above all else to see a return to the days of German prestige, honour and power. A key plank of his vision was the immediate return of territory lost to the Reich. This was to prove the major motivating factor that shaped Hitler's actions for the next five years.

The former Allies presented a major obstacle to the ambitions that Hitler may have harboured in his desire to recover the territories taken from Germany. The German armed forces had not been fully modernized nor were they yet equipped with an abundance of the latest weapons. The Allies collectively controlled an industrial and possessed military base which was infinitely stronger than Germany's. Britain had the preponderance of sea power and could rely upon the population and material resources of its worldwide empire for support. France had the largest reservoir of trained manpower in Western Europe by reason of its conscription program. Moreover, France had made defensive arrangements with Romania and the postwar states of Czechoslovakia and Yugoslavia, in addition to its alliance with Poland.

Despite these huge advantages Britain and France had suffered greatly in World War I and were reluctant to engage in another armed conflict with Germany. This made them reluctant to compel compliance with the territorial changes made in 1919 especially those changes that raised complex local issues such as those in Upper Silesia, which in any event were not absolutely essential to the Allies own vital interests. Hitler correctly gauged this extreme reluctance on the part of the former Allied nations to engage in military action, and as a result his foreign policy took the form a dangerous game of bluff.

The Inter War Reichsheer

Hitler had to be extremely careful in his dreams of military expansion however as the military clauses of the Versailles Treaty in 1919 strictly limited the German armed forces and permitted the establishment to a small 100,000 strong army composed of long-term volunteers. Conscription and universal training were prohibited, and the possession of major offensive weapons including aircraft, tanks, and submarines, were not permitted. The draconian provisions of the treaty of Versailles on the Reichsheer called for a twelve-year period of enlistment for landsers (private soldiers) and NCOs. Army officers were to be required to serve for a period of twenty-five years, which limited the ability of the Reichsheer to train a wider cadre for the job of command. A further stipulation by the Allies meant that no more than five percent of the officers and enlisted personnel could be released yearly. This ensured that opportunities to gain military experience and knowledge was strictly limited. These clever requirements and the prohibition against conscription and universal training effectively prevented the formation of a reserve of any size. Further more no field pieces larger than 105mm were to be allowed. The exception was for a few fixed guns of heavier calibre sited in the old fortress of Koenigsberg, in East Prussia. One other humiliating provision was that the detailed organization and proposed armament of all German units formed had first to be approved by the Allies.

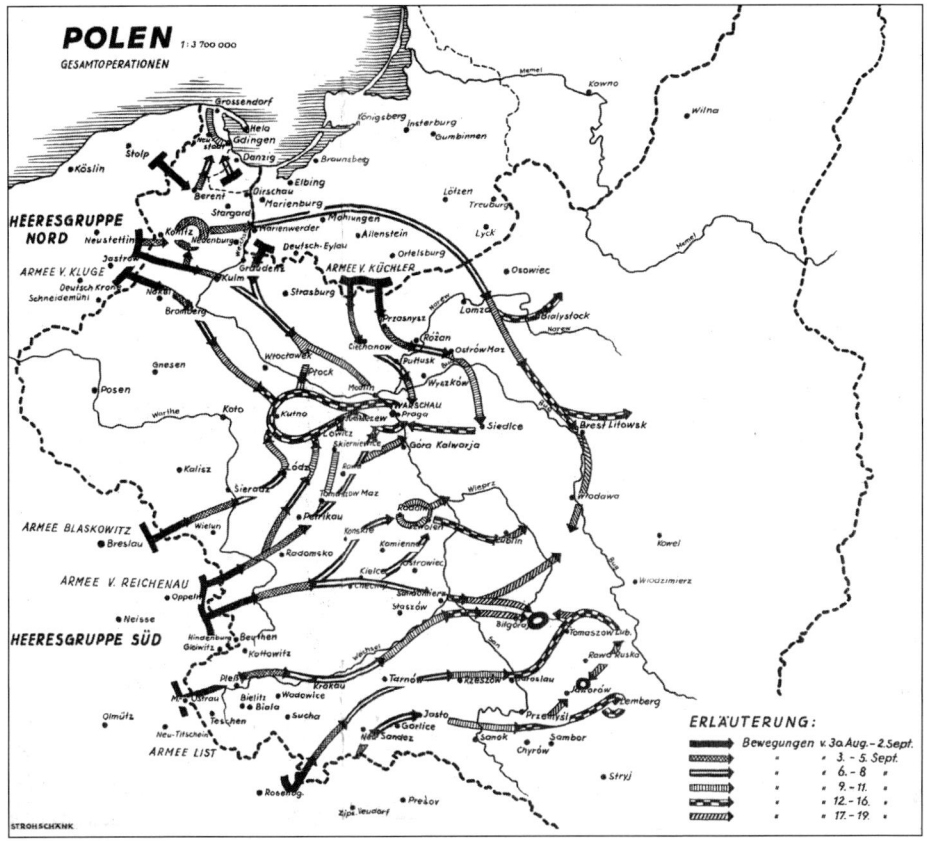

Map of Poland during the German advance

The new German military organization could therefore be little more than a police and coastal patrol force, incapable of carrying out any aggressive action outside the Reich. Even as a defensive organization, the postwar armed forces would require considerable reinforcement to protect the Reich in the event of war with one or more of its stronger neighbours.

The Polish-German non-aggression pact

In order to minimize the risks of an armed conflict while he executed his first designs in Europe, the new German dictator felt it necessary to effect a rapprochement with Poland. We will never know whether or not Hitler was simply buying time, but there is at least some evidence that his intentions were genuine in this respect. On 26th January 1934 the Polish and German Governments announced the signing of a pact binding both to solving their differences by arbitration. The agreement was to be in effect for ten years, unless renounced six months in advance by either of the contracting parties. In his justification of the agreement that was broadcast to the German people, Hitler claimed that he had entered into the pact to prevent the crystallization of bad feelings over the boundaries and to prevent a flare up into the traditional enmity that existed between the Germans and Poles. Relations with Poland had been very bad at the time the National Socialist government was established, and Hitler needed time and as he was too weak to act in any other way. In 1934 he had no option and on the surface appeared to genuinely desire to improve relations with Poland in the a peaceful manner until such time as he felt himself strong enough to act.

The build up and modernisation of German forces took a number of years and throughout that period Hitler continued to underline the importance of the Polish–German pact. On 30th January 1937 Hitler once again reaffirmed the importance of the pact to the assembled Reichstag, declaring it instrumental in easing tension between the two countries. However, since making the original agreement, Germany had openly renounced the terms of the Versailles treaty, reintroduced conscription and greatly expanded its Army. A fledgling Air Force had been organized, new warships constructed, and the beginnings of an undersea fleet created. Hitler's first great gamble had gone uncontested when Germany had remilitarized the Rhineland in March of 1936 without any form of intervention by the allies, and National Socialist agitators were stirring up trouble in Austria and Czechoslovakia, both were soon to feel the pressure of Hitler's demands.

The Austrian and Czechoslovak crises

Hitler gave the Poles reason to be apprehensive over his wider intentions. Throughout the remainder of 1937 and into late 1938 he was fully occupied in his machinations to gain control of Austria and of Czechoslovakia's Sudetenland. The Sudetenland had been part of Austria prior to World War I and was inhabited by a German-speaking population. Austria of course was the birthplace of the Fuhrer.

In Austria Hitler and the local Nazis had long been playing a game of political cat and mouse with the moderate Austrian government. The National Socialists unexpectedly gained the political edge in February 1938 when the anti-Nazi Austrian Chancellor, Dr. Kurt Schuschnigg, was finally forced to take the National Socialist Dr. Arthur Seyss-Inquart into his cabinet. He was appointed Minister of the Interior which gave Seyss-Inquart control of the police and paved the way for the Anschluss. Hitler immediately accelerated his war of nerves in Austria, and in March 1938 Dr. Schuschnigg, reluctant to bring on war, resigned in favour of Seyss-Inquart. With the Austrian Nazis now in power German troops marched into the country unopposed. The Republic of Austria was dissolved and its territory incorporated into the Third Reich.

The annexation of Austria increased considerably the German threat to Czechoslovakia. Prior to World War I the Sudetenland had been part of Austria. Konrad Henlein's Sudeten German Party justifiably claimed to represent Czechoslovakia's three million ethnic Germans and it was they clamoured for autonomy and union with the Reich. During the summer of 1938 the pro-Nazi elements among the Czech Germans demanded that the Sudetenland should be allowed to secede from Czechoslovakia Hitler held out the promise of German military intervention a move that, in the absence of support from their allies or Great Britain, the Czechs could really hope not resist. Nonetheless Hitler's threatening attitude caused the Prague government to order full mobilization in September 1938. War appeared imminent. British and French attempts to enlist the support of the Soviet Union were unavailing and without the help of the Soviets neither Britain or France had the appetite for war with Germany. On 29th September 1938 the British, French and Italians met with Hitler at Munich to hear his demands in relation to the cessation of the Sudetenland. Czechoslovakia was not represented at the meeting, but an agreement was nonetheless reached which granted the German leader's demands.

The Czechoslovak government, urged by Britain and France, meekly accepted the stipulations lay down by Hitler. The alternative undoubtedly would certainly have been war, but without the Soviets Britain and France simply did not have the stomach for the prospect of war at that point in time. Without the prospect of British or French military support Czechoslovakia was incapable of effective resistance and therefore had no choice but to accede to German demands however unreasonable. This craven and cowardly act was famously hailed by Chamberlain as the harbinger of "peace in our time." The adoption of the policy appeasement of which the Munich Agreement was the shameful culmination of the Allied refusal to confront Nazi aggression.

The text of the Agreement reached on September 29, 1938, between Germany, the United Kingdom, France, and Italy reads as follows;

Germany, the United Kingdom, France, and Italy, taking into consideration the agreement, which has been already reached in principle for the cession to Germany of the Sudeten German territory, have agreed on the following terms and conditions governing the said cession and the measures consequent thereon, and by this agreement they each hold themselves responsible for the steps necessary to secure its fulfillment.

1) The evacuation will begin on 1st October.

2) The United Kingdom, France, and Italy agree that the evacuation of the territory shall be completed by 10th October, without any existing installations having been destroyed, and that the Czechoslovak Government will be held responsible for carrying out the evacuation without damage to the said installations.

3) The conditions governing the evacuation will be laid down in detail by an international commission composed of representatives of Germany, the United Kingdom, France, Italy, and Czechoslovakia.

4) The occupation by stages of the predominantly German territory by German troops will begin on October 1st. The four territories marked on the attached map will be occupied by German troops in

Hitler in 1937 at the time this picture was taken the Fürher was aware of how limited his forces were was still regularly reinforcing the importance of the Germano-Polish peace pact signed in 1934.

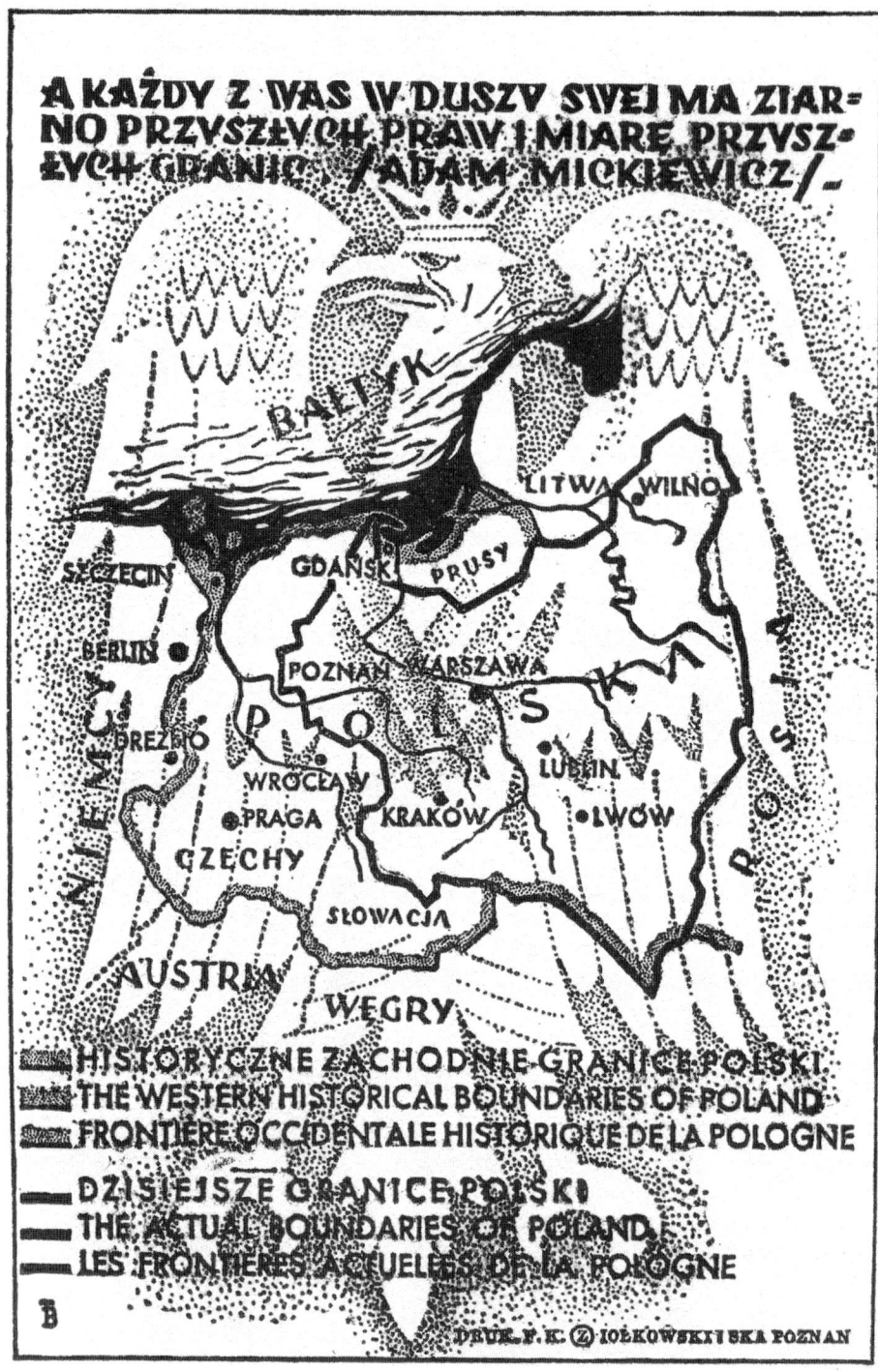

The border of Poland in 1939 contrasted with the fullest extent of the Polish state in the eighteenth century when Polish territory stretched well in to Brandenberg.

the following order: the territory marked number I on the 1st and 2nd of October, the territory marked number II on the 2nd and 3rd of October, the territory marked number III on the 3rd, 4th, and 5th of October, the territory marked number IV on the 6th and 7th of October. The remaining territory of preponderantly German character will be ascertained by the aforesaid international commission forthwith and be occupied by German troops by the 10th of October.

5) The international commission referred to in paragraph 3 will determine the territories in which a plebiscite is to be held. These territories will be occupied by international bodies until the plebiscite has been completed. The same commission will fix the conditions in which the plebiscite is to be held, taking as a basis the conditions of the Saar [territory ceded to France by the treaty of Versailles for 15 years; returned to Germany in 1935] plebiscite. The commission will also fix a date, not later than the end of November, on which the plebiscite will be held.

6) The final determination of the frontiers will be carried out by the international commission. This commission will also be entitled to recommend to the four Powers, Germany, the United Kingdom, France, and Italy, in certain exceptional cases, minor modifications in the strictly ethnographical determination of the zones which are to be transferred without plebiscite.

7) There will be a right of option into and out of the transferred territories, the option to be exercised within six months from the date of this agreement. A German-Czechoslovak commission shall determine the details of the option, consider ways of facilitating the transfer of population and settle questions of principle arising out of the said transfer.

8) The Czechoslovak Government will, within a period of four weeks from the date of this agreement, release from their military and police forces any Sudeten Germans who may wish to be released, and the Czechoslovak Government will within the same period release Sudeten German prisoners who are serving terms of imprisonment for political offences.

Adolf Hitler
Ed. Daladier
Mussolini
Neville Chamberlain
Munich, September 29, 1938

By the provisions of the agreement, Czechoslovak forces evacuated the Sudeten areas between 1st and 10th October 1938. Scheduled plebiscites were not held, and Germany took control of areas with a total population of 3.5million, of whom 700,000 were Czechs. Fortifications, which would have made a German invasion difficult if not impossible at the time, were turned over to the German Army intact.

Poland took advantage of the opportunity afforded by the Munich agreement to regain the remainder of the Teschen industrial area which had been seized by Czechoslovakia at the time Czechoslovakia and Poland were formed. Polish troops moved into the Teschen region on 2nd October 1938, taking control of 400 square miles of territory and a population of

Adolf Hitler and Joseph Goebbels at Horst Wessel's grave in Berlin in 1933.

240,000 of mixed Czech and Polish origin. On 2nd November 1938 Hungary too took advantage of the turmoil and seized 5,000 square miles of southern Slovakia, an area that Hungary had lost to Czechoslovakia in 1919, with a population of one million. Both Polish and Hungarian acquisitions were condoned by Germany and Italy.

Within Czechoslovakia itself, there was another deep encroachment on the state's sovereignty and territorial integrity. A strong separatist movement in Slovakia forced the government to grant autonomy to the Slovaks, under Joseph Tiso, and the name of the State was changed to Czecho-Slovakia. Territorial losses and establishment of a large autonomous area within a weak federal system combined to make Czecho-Slovakia a rump state, almost powerless to repel invasion. Tiso and a number of other leaders were quite frank about their close ties with Germany.

The revival of German claims against Poland

Poland had been quick to grab her territory back from the Czechs in 1938 but she was about to play a similar game with an altogether deadlier adversity and this time they would be on the receiving end of the demands. With the Czechoslovak question settled for the time being, Hitler was free to turn his attention to Poland and events moved swiftly. On 24th October 1938 Joachim von Ribbentrop, the Reich Foreign Minister, made a series of requests that re-opened the dispute over the Corridor and soon precipitated a new crisis. The German proposals involved the return of Danzig to Germany, but in return assured for Poland railway, port, and other economic facilities. One fairly reasonable request was that Poland should permit the construction of an extraterritorial road and railroad across the Corridor. In return for these concessions, Germany would guarantee the Polish-German frontiers and extend the nonaggression pact for as long as 25 years.

Pilsudski had warned his countrymen years earlier that the German attitude toward Danzig would be an indication of Germany's true intentions toward Poland and Polish public opinion would never condone the surrender of Poland's sovereignty in part of the Corridor. The diplomatic world was not surprised when Poland firmly rejected the German offer.

In March 1939 a series of significant events in Czechoslovakia further strengthened the German position in the controversy with Poland. These events began with the dismissal of Tiso from office by the Prague government for allegedly scheming to take Slovakia out of the federal union. Tiso was supported by Hitler, and President Hacha was summoned to Berlin and induced to place Czecho-Slovakia under German protection. Slovakia was granted full independence and Carpatho-Ukraine was annexed by Hungary. Bohemia and Moravia, all that remained of the truncated Czechoslovak state, were occupied by German troops on 15th March. A German official was appointed Protector of Bohemia and Moravia, with President Hacha retained as the nominal Chief of State. Czechoslovakia ceased to exist. A day later Tiso requested that Hitler also place Slovakia under German protection, and agreed to grant German troops passage to certain frontier areas. This arrangement would enable Germany to use Slovak territory as a base of operations against Poland from the south in the event of hostilities.

The establishment of the protectorate and Hitler's proclamation in Prague that Bohemia and Moravia belonged to the German lebensraum (living space) made obvious to the world the extent of National Socialist ambitions. For the first time Hitler had gone beyond his irredentist claims and swallowed up an area with a predominantly non-German population. British Prime Minister Neville Chamberlain, hitherto an advocate of appeasement, stated two days later that this latest acquisition had raised the question of German domination of the world. From this point British determination to contain Hitler gained support

The Fuhrer however carried on regardless. On 23rd March 1939 Lithuania acceded to German demands for the Memelland, a small strip of former Reich territory along Lithuania's southwestern frontier. The following day Germany and Romania concluded an economic agreement whereby the Germans would acquire almost the entire output of Romania's extensive oil industry. This partially resolved a pressing problem for the conduct of military operations by the German Armed Forces.

On 31st March Chamberlain addressed the British House of Commons, stating that Britain and France would assist Poland in the event Poland were attacked. The British and French Governments had reached an understanding, and Britain was to act as spokesman for the two nations. The issue of peace or war was left for Germany and Poland to decide.

Hitler would not permit much further delay in arriving at a solution of the territorial controversy favourable to Germany. The Poles, for their part, were determined to reject all German demands, since it was apparent to them that any concession would mean sharing the fate that had befallen Czechoslovakia. The die was now cast and there was every chance of peace or war.

CHAPTER 3

The Eve Of War

The diplomatic and military events that preceded hostilities were closely interrelated. Hitler now felt strong enough to hang the threat of military action over the Poles in order to obtain the concessions he sought concerning Danzig and the Corridor. The Poles were not fooled they shrewdly reckoned that these apparently reasonable requests would only be the thin end of a wedge leading to the return of the entire corridor and the situation understandably became increasingly tense.

It was obvious from the outset that the Poles could not be intimidated. The Warsaw government remained firm in its refusal to cede Polish rights in Danzig or sovereignty in The Corridor area. Hitler then resolved to dissuade the British and French from their stand in support of the Poles but he was now adamant that he would settle the problem by force if necessary.

A statement of Hitler's intentions was made to Keitel as chief of OKW and von Brauchitsch as commander in chief of the Army on 25th March 1939. On this day the Führer instructed these officers to initiate preparations for a solution of the problem of Poland by military means. This involved a gamble on the part of Hitler, since he had no understanding with the British and French as he had the preceding year at Munich during the Czech crisis. Moreover, the western nations were now alive to the danger posed by Hitler and might intervene to stop further German expansion. Hitler's racial theories and his anti-Semitic policy had done Germany irreparable harm in the public opinion of the western world.

German and Polish propaganda agencies were already engaged in a noisy campaign against one another. Stories of atrocities against the German minority in The Corridor were given wide dissemination in film and print. Germans arriving from Poland as volunteers for the armed forces or Reich Labor Service related further incidents of anti-German activities beyond the border.

Much also hinged on the circle of Hitler's chief lieutenants during this period. Joachim von Ribbentrop was not a career diplomat his background was in wine sales. As Foreign Minister he was blunt and tactless and in consequence had incurred considerable ill will abroad; Ribbentrop's threatening manner and lack of tact appeared typical of Germany's foreign policy. Moreover, Ribbentrop completely underestimated the British and their determination to honor their obligation to Poland.

Other members of Hitler's inner circle were also hard at work. Goering continued to build up an offensive air force. Josef Goebbels had organized a highly effective propaganda machine for the furtherance of National Socialist policies. A pliable Nazi cipher had been found in the form of Walter Funk, who succeeded Hjalmar Schacht as Minister of Economics

Hitler greets Chamberlain and Ribbentrop on 13th September 1938 during the Sudetenland crisis. Ribbentrop soon moved the focus from Czechoslovakia to Poland. This time Chamberlain would not be fooled and war was the inevitable result

who was replaced when he had shown the audacity to warn Hitler against his reckless military expenditure. The chiefs of the armed services were in no position to oppose any premature military adventures the Führer might entertain.

Fall Weiss

Part II of OKW's "Directive for the Armed Forces, 1939-40" was issued on 3rd April and in part it formed Hitler's reply to Chamberlain's pledge of support to Poland made in the House of Commons three days earlier. Part II was entitled "FALL WEISS" (Plan White), and its issue before the rest of the directive proper attested to its urgency. FALL WEISS opened with a brief discussion (drafted by Hitler himself) of relations with Poland. The attitude of Poland might require a solution by force, so preparations were to be made by 1st September to settle the problem for all time. Should war occur, the Wehrmacht would have the mission of destroying Poland's armed forces by surprise attack. To preserve secrecy, mobilization would not be ordered until immediately before the attack. The Army would establish contact between East Prussia and the Reich at the beginning of operations, and could utilize Slovak territory.

It was specified that only active units would be used in the opening attack, and these would be moved into concentration areas in the frontier region on Hitler's order. The Navy would destroy or neutralize the Polish fleet and merchant marine, blockade Polish ports, and secure sea communication with East Prussia. The Luftwaffe would destroy the Polish Air

A view from the cockpit of a Heinkel 111 in flight over the Polish countryside

Force, disrupt Polish mobilization, and render the Army close support.

Fall Weiss also took the Western Allies into consideration, since these were believed to be the greater threat to Germany. Measures were to be taken to secure the West wall, the North and Baltic Sea areas, and the air defence of Germany. Poland would be isolated, and a quick conquest would preclude external assistance.

The covering letter, signed by Keitel, stated that a timetable of preparations was to be made by OKW. The three services were directed to submit their campaign plans and recommendations for this timetable by 1st May 1939. These would be coordinated by OKW, and differences among the Army, Navy, and Air Force would be worked out in joint conferences.

Parts I and III of the directive, issued separately on 11th April 1939, were recapitulations of instructions included in the directive for the preceding year. Part I gave detailed instructions for defensive arrangements on Germany's frontiers. Part III restated a previous plan to seize Danzig without war. The extent of defensive preparations would depend upon the situation with Germany's neighbours. As for Danzig, it might be possible to seize the city from East Prussia should a diplomatic situation favourable to Germany develop.

Part IV consisted of special instructions to the commander of I Corps in East Prussia. In effect, in the event of war, I Corps would provide personnel for the headquarters of Third Army, and the army commander would be responsible for the defence of the exposed German province.

Part V of the annual directive determined the boundaries for the theatres of operations in the east and west. Part VI was of particular concern to the German war economy. While protecting its own war industries and sources of supply, Germany was to utilize those production centers it could capture intact and would limit damage in operations to the minimum. In connection with Plan WEISS, the industrial areas of Poland centring on Cracow and Teschen were of particular importance.

A special annex to the directive, issued on 21st April, specified that there would be no declaration of war in implementing Fall Weiss. A partial mobilization of reserves might be required but this would not necessarily involve the mobilization of industry. However, in the event of a general war, both reserves and industry would be mobilized immediately.

The issuance of the "Directive for the Armed Forces, 1939-40" initiated preparations to resolve the matter of German claims against Poland. Germany might be able to exert sufficient pressure on the Poles to obtain Danzig and special privileges in The Corridor, or might seize Danzig by surprise. If neither of these was successful, Hitler might direct the implementation of Plan WEISS, a solution by force. Defensive measures to be taken in the west would secure Germany against attack by Britain and France while differences with Poland were being settled. The preparations in the first two months following the issuance of the directive were concerned mostly with planning the movement of units and logistical installations into position to launch an overwhelming attack against Poland should the Führer decide upon the alternative of war.

Diplomatic developments, April-July

On 28th April 1939 Hitler abrogated the Polish-German Non-aggression Pact of 1934 and the London Naval Agreement of 1935 in a Reichstag speech. Hitler had for some time pursued an aggressive program of diplomacy in respect of Poland and when Germany unilaterally withdrew from both agreements the die was now cast. In early 1939, Hitler had already issued orders to prepare for a possible "solution of the Polish problem by military means." Hitler also stated further that the issue of Danzig must be settled immediately.

Agitators were covertly sent into Danzig to embarrass and annoy the Polish government. Polish flags were torn down and Polish property was damaged on 12th May, the anniversary of Pilsudski's death. Shortly afterward a Polish customs house was attacked. Polish measures against the German population in Danzig and The Corridor were given wide publicity in the German press and broadcasts, and Danzig's National Socialist faction, dominating the city government, clamoured for reunion with the Reich.

A pact with the Italians on 22nd May 1939 brought Mussolini into Hitler's camp. As usual Mussolini was less than whole hearted. Italian participation involved no military support, and the Italian dictator was even assured that there would be no war for the next several years. The advantage to Germany lay in obtaining a secure flank to the south and preventing an agreement

Ethnic Germans in the Sudetenland express their delight at being re-united with the Reich.

Although the process of mechanisation was well underway in 1939, the German Army was still heavily reliant on horse power.

between Italy and the Allies. Italy on France's eastern frontier would neutralize part of the large French Army, and Britain's naval position and the Suez Canal would be threatened by the Italian fleet.

The focus for diplomatic scene now shifted to Moscow. In the early summer of 1939 Britain and France were attempting to enlist the aid of the Soviet Union in presenting a solid front to Germany. Negotiations were slow, and the Russians refused to commit themselves to any coalition agreement. Meanwhile, in Berlin, Hitler received formal visits from the Hungarian Prime Minister, Regent Paul of Yugoslavia, and the Prime Minister of Bulgaria. Each of these visits featured military demonstrations designed to display of Germany's armed power to a watching world.

Germany's strong diplomatic position at this point required one more support to discourage British and French intervention and assure Hitler a free hand in Poland- the collaboration, or at least the friendly neutrality, of the Soviet Union. Hitler would forsake his own long-standing anti-Communist policy by such a step, but a rapprochement with the Russians would be welcomed in wide diplomatic and military circles in Germany. Ribbentrop favoured an arrangement of this nature, as did the German Ambassador in Moscow, Count von der Schulenberg.

The Russians had already indicated a desire to normalize and improve relations with Germany the preceding April, when their Chargé d'Affaires had approached a representative of the German Foreign Office in the course of discussions on commercial matters.

Hitler seized upon the opportunity to settle outstanding differences and offered the

Russians uncontested domination of Latvia and Estonia, Poland east of Warsaw and the Vistula from Warsaw to the south, thence east of the San River, in exchange for a free hand west of that line. The Russians, willing to bargain with Hitler in Polish, Lithuanian, Latvian, and Estonian soil and lives, accepted the offer.

Events, 1st-22nd August

Disorders in Danzig and the Polish Corridor became increasingly serious during the first three weeks of August, and German pressure against the Poles was intensified. Britain and France repeated their assurances to the Polish Government, and the attitude of the Western Allies served to strengthen Polish determination to resist German demands. Concluding that time was working to his disadvantage, the Führer hastened in his course. German military concentrations in the east, though camouflaged as manoeuvres, grew more threatening as the diplomatic situation deteriorated.

Danzig was infiltrated by German agents and military personnel in civilian clothing throughout August. The police were openly anti-Polish and assisted the Germans in organizing military forces inside the city. Forster, head of the National Socialist Party in Danzig, made no secret of his visits to Hitler and his aim of incorporating the Free City into the Reich. The increasing seriousness of the situation and the denial of its commercial rights by the city administration caused the Polish Government to take measures of reprisal in the nature of embargoes, giving the Germans more propaganda material for consumption in the Reich. Other incidents were touched off in The Corridor border areas.

An attempt to dissuade Hitler was made by Count Galeazzo Ciano, Mussolini's Foreign Minister, in a conference with Hitler and Ribbentrop on 12th and 13th August. Mussolini was not ready for war and desired a period of several years in which Italy might recover from its military ventures in Ethiopia, Spain, and Albania. The Italian services required reorganization and modern equipment and would not be ready for the field until 1942 or later. Hitler was adamant, however, and Ciano left the meeting thoroughly embittered at the German breach of faith.

Preparations for the incident necessary to give Germany a pretext for invading Poland were made on 17th August, when the Wehrmacht was ordered to supply Reinhard Heydrich, deputy to Heinrich Himmler, with Polish uniforms. The purpose of this was to create incidents wherein German soil would be violated by persons identified as members of the Polish Armed Forces. Hitler would then be in position to claim that he was justified in ordering the Wehrmacht to defend German territory, lives, and property, and in moving forces into Poland to restore order in a situation that the Polish government could not control.

Hitler in triumph mode as he leads a procession through the flower strewn streets of the Sudetenland, At this point it seemed to the German people that the Führer could do no wrong.

Hitler held a conference with his service chiefs, the commanders of the major forces being deployed against Poland, and the chief of OKW on 22nd August. The Führer's speech was a rambling monologue lasting for hours. In substance, he felt that the time was ripe to resolve German differences with Poland by war and to test the Reich's new military machine. It was unlikely that Britain and France would intervene; if they did, Germany would be able to carry on a long war if necessary. Britain and France had promised Poland support, but were in no position to render material aid of any consequence. Moreover, Hitler felt, the British and French leaders would hesitate to draw their respective nations into a general war.

There was also another vitally important factor to be considered. The Russians were about to sign a non-aggression pact with the Germans. Ribbentrop had left for Moscow earlier that day, to obtain the signature of Foreign Commissar Molotov to the agreement already worked out by German and Russian representatives. Stalin was no friend of the Poles and the agreement with him would strengthen the German economic front considerably.

According to Hitler, an appropriate "incident" would be used to justify the German attack on Poland. The morality of such a device was inconsequential. Victory was all that mattered. Hitler closed his address with an assurance to the assembled commanders that he was certain the armed services could accomplish any task set for them.

Sixteen years earlier Hitler had outlined in his book Mein Kampf the program on which he was about to embark. In this rambling account of his early struggles and his philosophy, Hitler had stated that future efforts at German expansion would be directed toward the east, to the Soviet Union and the states dominated (according to Hitler) by Moscow. He had also

German infantry advance through the ruins of a Polish village.

Adolf Hitler with the Reichstag delegates in 1939.

The Battleship Schleswig Holstein opens fire on the Westerplatte.

discussed the matter of an alliance with the Soviet Union and had stated that it would mean war, since Britain and France would not wait a decade until the new coalition became too strong for them to defeat. Instead, Britain and France would move against the Reich immediately. The Führer had also charged the Soviet leaders as criminals, with no intention of honouring the obligations they would incur by an alliance. Hitler's actions from this point were to reveal his utter cynicism. The German dictator was fully aware of the risk of bringing on a general war, despite the assurances to his military leaders that there would be no war with the west over Poland.

The pact with the Russians

An ominous step towards the fate that would befall Poland was the signing of the Molotov-Ribbentrop Pact on 23rd August 1939. The secret Nazi-Soviet talks held in Moscow succeeded partially as a result of the vacuum left by France and Britain's own failure to secure an alliance with the Soviet Union. With the signing of the protocol Germany avoided the prospect of Soviet intervention in Hitler's planned campaign against Poland. The public announcement of the 23rd August 1939 agreement with the Soviet Union only told half of the story but it exploded all hopes of a peaceful settlement between Germany and Poland. In that part of the document made public, the Soviet Union and Germany made a simple statement of non-aggression, which meant that the Russians would not intervene on the side of Poland were that country to be attacked by Germany. In a sinister secret protocol to this pact, the Germans and the Soviets also agreed to divide Eastern Europe, including Poland, into two spheres of influence; the western third of the country was to go to Germany and the remainder to the Soviet Union and established the line of the Narew, Vistula, and San Rivers as the boundary between the German and Soviet spheres of interest in Poland. It was also agreed that Finland, Estonia, and Latvia would fall within the Russian sphere of influence, while Lithuania would fall within the German sphere of interest. The signing of the pact did have its disadvantages and served to alienate the Japanese.

Mussolini decided to remain aloof from the diplomatic turmoil. However, the Italian dictator saw the beginning of a realization of further Italian designs on the Balkan Peninsula should the war spread. Mussolini already held Albania and coveted portions of Yugoslavia and Greece.

On 24th August 1939 the British gave written guarantees to Poland, obligating both Britain and France to come to the aid of Poland in the event Germany launched an attack. This unexpected development, when it came to the attention of the Reich government the following day, caused Hitler to rescind the order he had given to commence operations against Poland on 26th August. The Führer immediately set about to deter the British and French by an offer of German guarantees to support the British Empire and respect existing frontiers with France. Neither Britain nor France were moved by Hitler's offer. Poland was shunted aside, and Hitler dealt with the British representatives as spokesmen for the Polish Government as well as the French from this point. The German assault on Poland as envisaged by Fall Weiss was originally scheduled to begin at 04:00 on August 26th 1939. However, the Polish-British Common Defence Pact was now signed as an annex to the Franco-Polish Military Alliance. Under the terms of the pact both countries committed to the preservation of Polish independence. On signing the accord, Britain committed to providing immediate military support in the defence of Poland in the event of a German attack. Despite the signing of the accord, in late August 1939 the British and the Poles were

The Westerplatte under fire from the Schleswig Holstein.

German marines storm ashore in the Westerplatte.

still desperate to avoid armed conflict and were openly suggesting to Berlin that both nations were prepared to resume genuine negotiations . Faced with this unexpected development Hitler's resolve briefly deserted him. After a series of uncontested successes in the Rhineland, Sudetenland, Austria and Czechoslovakia, in which Hitler's brinksmanship had paid off, his forces had finally been confronted by an adversary that was obviously prepared to fight if required. The Fuhrer therefore postponed his attack until 1st September 1939 though this meant halting the entire invasion as Hitler described it "in mid-leap".

On 26th August 1939, Hitler tried once more to dissuade the British and the French from interfering in the forthcoming conflict. Hitler even went as far as far as to suggest that, if a peaceful solution could be found ,Wehrmacht forces would be made available to assist Britain in defending her empire in the future. The strong British and French participation in these negotiations seems to converted Hitler to the view that in the event of an attack on Poland there was some prospect that the Western Allies would not actually wage war on Germany at all. Hitler mistakenly came to the view that the British might actually be willing to negotiate a compromise peace favourable to Germany in the wake of a successful conquest of Poland.

The reply to Hitler's offer to support the British Empire was delivered by the Ambassador in Berlin, Sir Nevile Henderson, on 28th August. Henderson reemphasized Britain's position in the event of German hostilities against Poland. Hitler gave no answer at the time, but promised Ambassador Henderson a reply the following day. At 1915 on 29th August the British Ambassador was informed that a Polish plenipotentiary would have to be in Berlin the following day, with full powers to negotiate a settlement. The Polish Ambassador was not present at these meetings, nor were Polish representatives invited to attend. Prompted by the British, Germany issued one last diplomatic offer. With Fall Weiss still not rescheduled, at midnight on August 29th, German Foreign Minister Joachim von Ribbentrop handed British Ambassador Sir Neville Henderson the list of terms designed to ensure peace with regard to Poland. Danzig was to be returned to Germany (Gdynia would remain with Poland), and there was to be a plebiscite in the Polish Corridor, based on residency in 1919. This was to take place within the year. An exchange of minority populations between the two countries was also proposed. It was peremptorily ordered that a Polish plenipotentiary was to arrive in Berlin and accept these terms by noon the next day. In reality the German proposal was all but impossible. The British Ambassador had first to inform his government of the Reich's most recent demand, and the British Government would have to send the message to the Polish Government, which in turn would have to give one individual full authority to sign any agreement put forth by the Germans. The plenipotentiary would also have to be in the Reich capital by midnight of 30th August. The German demands had also been expanded to include a plebiscite in the entire Corridor region on a return to the Reich, in addition to the outright return of Danzig.

The Poles sensed that the end game had arrived and in recognition of their inferior position the Polish Navy wisely sent its destroyer flotilla to Britain in a secret operation code named Operation Peking. On the same day, Marshal of Poland Edward Rydz-Śmigły announced the mobilization of Polish troops. However, he was pressured into revoking the order by the French, who still hoped for a diplomatic settlement, failing to realize that the Germans were fully mobilized and concentrated at the Polish border.

The Molotov-Ribbentrop Pact is signed in Moscow.

The British Cabinet viewed the terms of the German offer as "reasonable", except the demand for the urgent plenipotentiary, which the British viewed as an unacceptable form of ultimatum. Accordingly Britain and urged the 2 main protagonists to continue talking. When Polish Ambassador Lipski went to see Ribbentrop early in the evening of 30th August Ribbentrop received the Polish Ambassador, but as the latter was not empowered to act as plenipotentiary for his government the meeting accomplished nothing. When Lipski announced that he did not have the full power to sign, Ribbentrop dismissed him. The same evening the German Government broadcast its demands against Poland and blamed the

A barrage balloon on the eastern border of Poland and Germany.

breakdown in negotiation on the intransigence of Warsaw.

Ribbentrop now stated that the time limit allowed the Poles had expired. The German Foreign Minister read off the demands of his government to Ambassador Henderson, without benefit of translation, and furnished no copy of his text to either British or Polish representatives, as diplomatic practice required. Ribbentrop then announced in any event that negotiations were at an end.

On the following day, 31st August, Hitler signed "Directive No. 1 for the Conduct of the War". The time for the attack on Poland was set for 0445 the next morning; 1st September 1939. Neutrals were to be scrupulously respected and hostilities in the

Himmler congratulating Hitler on his 50th birthday.

west would be initiated only by Britain and France. Any force crossing the German frontier in the course of military counteraction would require Hitler's personal approval, though combat aircraft might cross the border in defending the Reich against British and French air attacks in force. In the event retaliation against Britain should become necessary, Hitler reserved to himself the right to order air attacks against London.

Due to a miscommunication a number of units in the difficult terrain in the south some German units had launched attacks as originally planned . This potentially disastrous situation was excused by the Nazi propaganda machine on the false premise that Poles had been behind the provocation in the form of a cross border raid carried out by Slovakians. To provide additional cover and some shadow of justification of the action he was about to undertake, Hitler had his agents arrange a number of carefully prepared "incidents" in the Polish border area. At 20:00 hrs on 31st August, a band of men "captured" the radio station at Gleiwitz in German Silesia. A short broadcast in Polish followed, announcing an attack on Germany, at which point the "attackers" were driven off, leaving one dead man behind. The "casualties" for these incidents, provided from among condemned prisoners and clad in Polish uniforms, were killed or rendered unconscious by fatal injections, then shot and left to be found by German police. The responsibility for the Gleiwitz operation had been assigned by Heydrich to an SS official, Alfred Nau jocks. Despite its crudity, the Gleiwitz incident was to be used by Hitler in his charge that regular Polish forces had violated Reich territory and that German troops had been forced to return their fire.

On 31st August 1939, Hitler ordered hostilities against Poland to start at 4:45am the next morning. Due to the French insistence that Polish mobilization must be halted during the negotiations stoppage, Poland managed to mobilise only 70 percent of its planned forces, and many units were still forming or moving to their designated positions when the attack was unleashed.

The Westerplatte fortress in German hands.

CHAPTER 4

The German Military Situation

T he Panzer Divisions that streamed into Poland on 1st September 1939 had been created to utilize a new operational doctrine, which the world has come to know as "Blitzkrieg". Although the term was not in use in the German armed forces in 1939 it does encapsulate the concept of a new form of mobile warfare that was designed to bypass the static drudgery of the Great War. It was envisaged that the new Panzer divisions would act in co-ordination with other elements of the military, punching holes in the enemy line and isolating selected units, which would be encircled and destroyed. These armoured thrusts would be followed up by less mobile mechanized infantry and foot soldiers. The Luftwaffe provided both tactical and strategic air power, particularly dive-bombers that disrupted lines of supply and communications. It was only later that the new method of mechanized would become widely known as Blitzkrieg. One of the distinguished historians who later seized on the term was Basil Liddell Hart who concluded that "Poland was a full demonstration of the Blitzkrieg theory."

The Panzer divisions

The five Panzer divisions varied in their components. The 1st, 2nd, and 3rd boasted one tank and one motorized infantry brigade. Each tank brigade had a paper strength of 561 machines including command tanks but none were up to strength for the Polish campaign; the 4th Panzer Division was particularly under equipped and comprised a tank brigade and just one regiment of motorized infantry. Like the tanks the motorized infantry were in short supply; the 5th Panzer Division consisted of a tank brigade and two ordinary infantry regiments. In addition, each Panzer division had a motorized artillery regiment with two battalions of 105mm howitzers; a reconnaissance battalion with motorcycle and armoured car companies; an antitank battalion with towed 37mm guns; an engineer battalion; a signal battalion; and rear trains and services. The authorized strength of the Panzer Division was approximately 12,000 officers and men, the variations in organization accounting meant that there were differences in personnel strength from one Panzer Division to the other.

Each Panzer Division fielded around 300 tanks across all four types then in service. Germany had a substantial numerical advantage over Poland and had developed a significant military prior to the conflict. The German invasion force fielded some 2,650 tanks organized into five Panzer Divisions, and four Motorized Infantry Divisions. The sheer number of vehicles produces the impression of a daunting display of military might, but the reality was less impressive.

The planners had allocated the 1st Panzer Division 56 Panzer Mark I, 78 Panzer Mark II,

Polish cavalry

112 Panzer Mark III, and 56 Panzer Mark IV tanks. The 2nd, 3rd, 4th, and 5th Panzer Divisions was each expected to have 124 Panzer Mark I, 138 Panzer Mark II, 20 Panzer Mark III, and 24 Panzer Mark IV tanks. In practice however these figures were never achieved, particularly in the case of the Panzer Mark III, which was in very short supply and could not supplied in the numbers required by the time the Panzer divisions took the field against Poland. The 4th Panzer Division received no Mark III tanks whatsoever.

There were also severe question marks over the quality of the vehicles especially the obsolete Panzer Mark I. This tiny vehicle was actually a two-man tankette, which weighed approximately six tons, and mounted two machine guns.

Surprisingly the Panzer I was actually one of the most common tanks employed in Poland despite the fact that this lightweight mini-Panzer was obviously under armed and offered very dubious armour protection. By 1939 The PzKpfw I was fit for training purposes only, but there was no alternative and 1,445 of these machines had to be deployed in the campaign.

The Panzer Mark II was not much of an improvement but unlike the Panzer I it at least mounted an armour piercing anti-tank gun albeit of very small calibre. The Mark II tank was a three-man vehicle that greatly increased the combat efficiency. It weighed twelve tons, and mounted a 20mm gun; 1,223 PzKpfw II light tanks were deployed in Poland. This under gunned and under armoured machine was effectively the main stay of the campaign.

The Panzer Mark III model had a crew of five, weighed approximately twenty four tons and had a more effective 37mm gun which was the equal of most enemy tanks then in service. This was a vastly superior machine to the Panzer II, but manufacturing delays meant that only 87 PzKpfw III were available for the campaign in Poland. The 4th Panzer Division got none and the 5th Panzer Division had to make do with only three vehicles.

The heaviest and best tank of the period was the Panzer Mark IV, which weighed 26 tons, carried a crew of five, and mounted a short-barreled 75mm gun. The PzKpfw IV was then the best battle tank in service and was to prove its value both in Poland and France. Unfortunately for the Wehrmacht only one hundred and ninety six of these new tanks were ready in time for the campaign.

In addition, there were 215 command tanks and other armoured vehicles including 202 ex-Czech light tanks that were designated PzKpfw 35(t). There were also seventy-eight examples of the Czech medium tank. A very acceptable vehicle which was designated PzKpfw 38(t). Along with tanks, there were some 308 heavy armoured cars, 718 light armoured cars along with 68 Sd.Kfz.251 medium armoured personnel carriers - a very useful cross country vehicle which was then only just entering service.

The light divisions

The four light divisions also varied in their organization, for example the 1st Light Division comprised a motorized infantry brigade of one regiment and a motorcycle battalion; the 2nd and 4th Light Divisions had two motorized infantry regiments each; and the 3rd Light Division had a motorized infantry regiment and a motorcycle battalion. Each of the light divisions had an organic light tank battalion, and the 1st Light Division had an organic tank regiment. The 1st Light Division had a reconnaissance battalion, while the 2nd, 3rd, and 4th

German horse-drawn artillery.

Polish infantry on the advance

Light Divisions had reconnaissance regiments. The division artillery of the light divisions was the same as that of the Panzer divisions, i.e. two light battalions of towed howitzers. Engineer, signal, and other normal attachments were similar to those of the infantry and Panzer divisions; all were motorized. The strength of the light division was approximately 11,000 officers and men.

The infantry divisions

The thirty-five active infantry divisions had three infantry regiments of three battalions, a cannon company, and an antitank company each. The battalions were four -company organizations, with the 4th, 8th and 12th companies (companies were numbered one through fourteen in the regiment) filling the role of heavy weapons companies in the comparable United States Army organization. The line (rifle) companies had a total of nine light and two heavy machine guns and three light (50mm) mortars each; the heavy weapons companies, eight heavy machine guns and six 81mm mortars each. As a matter of interest, the light and heavy machine guns were the same air-cooled weapon, model of 1934. With the bipod mount the MG 34, as it was known, was considered a light machine gun; with the tripod mount, it became a heavy machine gun. All transportation for the rifle and heavy weapons companies was horse drawn. The cannon company had six light (75mm) and two heavy (150mm) infantry howitzers. The anti-tank company had twelve 37mm towed guns and was the only completely motorized unit of the regiment. The reserve divisions were organized in similar fashion but their regiments lacked heavy infantry howitzers and the third and fourth wave divisions had obsolete machine guns from World War I.

The artillery element of the active infantry division was a mixed regiment of three light and one medium battalions, equipped with 105mm and 150mm howitzers, and an observation battalion. None of the reserve divisions had an observation battalion, and most of their firing battalions had obsolete artillery pieces from World War I.

Other divisional units for both active and reserve infantry divisions were a reconnaissance battalion; an antitank battalion with 37mm guns; an engineer battalion; a signal battalion; and rear trains and services. The total strength authorized the active infantry division was 17,875 officers and men. Wave II and IV divisions were smaller by 1,000 to 2,000 men or more, and Wave III divisions larger by approximately 600 men.

The four motorized infantry divisions were smaller than the active standard infantry divisions by approximately 1,400 men. Each of the motorized infantry divisions comprised three infantry regiments and was organized much as a standard division except that all elements of the division were transported by motor vehicle.

The three mountain divisions resembled the standard infantry divisions but were not organized uniformly. The 1st Mountain Division had three infantry regiments and four gun battalions in its artillery regiment; the 2nd and 3rd Mountain Divisions had only two regiments of infantry and three battalions of artillery apiece. The light mountain artillery battalions were equipped with 75mm pack guns, which could be dismantled and carried by mules, and the medium artillery battalions were equipped with 150mm howitzers of the type used by the infantry divisions. The authorized strength of the mountain division was approximately 17,000 officers and men, though the 1st Mountain Division for a time had a total strength of over 24,000 men.

Command organisation

General von Brauchitsch was still the Army's commander in chief in March 1939, with General der Artillerie Franz Haider as his chief of staff. The headquarters of the Army was known as the Oberkommando des Heeres (OKH), or the High Command of the Army.

For administration and other station complement functions OKH controlled 15 Wehrkreise, numbered I through XIII, XVII, and XVIII. Control over the Army's tactical forces was exercised through the six group commands.

Group Command 1, controlling the I, II, III, and VIII Corps, was in Berlin. Group Command 2 (Plan WEST) was at Frankfurt-am-Main and to it were attached the V, VI, and XII Corps, and the three frontier commands. Dresden was headquarters for Group Command 3, to which the IV, VII, and XIII Corps were responsible. Group Command 4 controlled the

A German tank in Graudenz

German infantry advancing in open order.

XIV Corps (motorized infantry divisions), XV Corps (light divisions), and XVI Corps (Panzer divisions), and was the forerunner of the Panzer armies of a later date; the headquarters of this group command was in Leipzig. Group Command 5 had its headquarters in Vienna, and controlled the XVII and XVIII Corps. Hannover was headquarters for Group Command 6, to which were attached the IX, X, and XI Corps. This peacetime subordination of corps would not necessarily pertain on mobilization, when the group commands became armies. As in the United States Army, corps in the German Army could be shifted from control of one army to the other.

The new Navy

Germany was permitted by terms of an agreement with the British on 18th June 1935 to build up to 35 percent of the latter's total naval tonnage and 45 percent of Britain's submarine tonnage. Following as it did on Hitler's denunciation of the military limitations imposed on the Reich by the Versailles Treaty, the naval agreement constituted tacit British consent to German rearmament. The British were temporarily reassured by the German agreement to limit the size of the Reich's new navy. However, the French were distressed by the increase in German naval power, and a wedge was driven in the Allied front.

By March 1939 the Hannover had been decommissioned and the obsolete battleships Schlesien and Schleswig-Holstein were being used as cadet training ships. Still armed, the old battleships could be used for secondary naval missions. The battle fleet proper was composed of the battleships Scharnhorst and Gneisenau; the three armoured cruisers (pocket battleships); two new heavy cruisers, the Bluecher and Admiral Hipper, displacing 10,000 tons and mounting 8-inch guns; the six light cruisers' built during the replacement construction program; 22 destroyers of the Maass and Boeder classes (1,625 and 1,811 tons), with 5-inch guns; and 43 submarines. The U- through U-24 and the U-56 displaced from 250 to 300 tons and were restricted to the coastal waters of the Baltic and North Seas. The U-25

Joseph Stalin overlooking the signing of the Molotov-Ribbentrop Pact by von Ribbentrop. The secret protocol allowed for the division of Poland between the Germans and the Soviets.

The Heinkel He-111 in production

and U-26 were 712-ton boats, and the U-37 through U-39 displaced 740 tons each; these larger submarines were capable of operating as far as mid-Atlantic without refueling. The U-27 through U-36 displaced 500 tons; the U-45, U-46, and U-51, 517 tons each. These last boats were capable of operations in the North Sea and the waters about the British Isles. Some additional submarines in various stages of construction would also be ready for operations by the outbreak of hostilities.

Admiral Raeder's Oberkommando der Kriegsmarine (OKM), or High Command of the Navy, controlled the fleet, Luftwaffe units attached to the Navy, and shore commands for the Baltic and North Sea coastal regions. The fleet comprised the heavy surface units, submarine arm, and naval reconnaissance forces. The shore commands were responsible for the training units and schools ashore, coast artillery units, arsenals, and other land installations of the Navy.

The new Air Force

The Luftwaffe by March 1939 was a potent attack force, which would have 4,303 operational aircraft available by the outbreak of hostilities. These would include 1,180 bombers, 336 dive-bombers, 1,179 fighters, 552 transports, 721 observation planes, 240 naval aircraft, and 95 miscellaneous airplanes. Aircraft played a major role in the campaign. Bombers also attacked cities, causing huge losses amongst the civilian population through terror bombing. A force of 2,315 aircraft was assigned to Fall Weiss. The Luftwaffe forces consisted of 1,180 fighter aircraft. 290 of these were the famous Ju 87 Stuka dive-bombers. Available in much greater numbers were the 1,100 conventional bombers mainly in the form of the He 111 although there were also a substantial force Dornier Do's. The Luftwaffe forces were completed by an assortment of 550 transport and 350 reconnaissance aircraft. As a result participation in the Spanish Civil War the Luftwaffe was the most experienced, best-trained and best-equipped air force in the world in 1939.

Goering's headquarters was known as the Oberkommando der Luftwaffe (OKL), or High Command of the Air Force. The four major subordinate air commands were designated as Luftflotten (air forces), and controlled both tactical and administrative units. This arrangement contrasted sharply with that of the Army, which had separate channels of command for its tactical and administrative components.

Tactical air units were dispersed about Germany in eight air divisions. The administrative commands, ten in number, were known as Luftgaue, similar to the Army's Wehrkreise, and provided the tactical air units with logistical support.

The organization of each air force was arranged to meet the particular needs of its respective mission. As a consequence, organization varied from one air force to the other. In general, each of the four air forces contained all types of aircraft in service, e.g. fighters, bombers, transports, and reconnaissance planes. The First Air Force had its headquarters in Berlin and responsibility for northern and eastern Germany. Braunschweig was the headquarters of the Second Air Force, dispersed over northwestern Germany. The Third Air Force, responsible for southwestern and southern Germany, was located in Munich. Vienna was headquarters for the Fourth Air Force, responsible for Austria and a portion of southeastern Germany. A separate tactical and administrative command of corps size was assigned to East Prussia and retained under OKL control.

The German military situation in March 1939

The power of the Wehrmacht, while formidable by early 1939, had been exaggerated by German and foreign news media out of proper proportion, and the Westwall was of limited value to the defence of the Reich. Five years was hardly sufficient time for the three services to build up and thoroughly integrate a large cadre of professional officers and noncommissioned officers. The crop of 250,000-300,000 Army conscripts that finished training each year was beginning to fill the reserve ranks, but training of the older men of the 1901-1913 age classes had lagged.

The active Army could be considered as one of the best trained in Europe, but lacked a sufficient number of qualified signal personnel and its Panzer forces were an untried experiment. The bulk of the tanks (Mark I and II) were known to be too light but could not be replaced at once with the heavier Mark III and Mark IV models. Rolling stock and truck transportation were in short supply and it would take time to organize additional reserve divisions and train the large number of men who had not yet seen service.

The Navy was far inferior in strength to the British Navy alone, and would be no match for the combined fleets of Britain and France. The German Navy had few capital ships, nor did it possess a sufficient number of destroyers to provide escort for the Reich's merchant vessels carrying critical materials from abroad. In the event of war, this meant that the large German merchant fleet would be restricted mainly to the North and Baltic Seas. The German submarine force, though it would soon equal the British in numbers, was much lighter in tonnage, and the range of many of the U-boats was restricted.

German cavalry on patrol

The German Air Force would experience no immediate problem insofar as personnel were concerned. The Luftwaffe's training program had turned out a sufficient number of pilots and aircrews to man an expanded wartime Air Force. For its part, German industry had provided the Luftwaffe with some of the most advanced operational aircraft of the day. The British and French Air Forces were larger, but a considerable number of their aircraft were obsolete or obsolescent. The Luftwaffe lacked airframe and engine replacements for sustained operations, however. Repair facilities, though well organized, were not nearly extensive enough for a major war effort.

Germany had an excellent industrial base for war, with its heavy plants in the Ruhr, Saar, and Silesian areas. According to the German planners, however, several more years were still needed to attain a production rate high enough to supply the materiel and ammunition for a major war. The military training program had already made inroads on the strength of the labor force, and mobilization would deprive it of additional thousands of technicians and workers who had completed their period of compulsory service and were assigned to reserve units.

In short, Germany was prepared only for a limited war of short duration. Gasoline and ammunition reserves would not suffice for simultaneous large-scale operations in the east and west, and the disaster of 1918 still acted to dampen the enthusiasm of the general public for military adventures. His series of successes in Austria and Czechoslovakia and the continued reluctance of Britain and France to take action, however, inclined Hitler to become more reckless. German military planning thus had to include numerous improvisations to meet sudden demands, a practice that was to become typical of the Reich's World War II operations.

CHAPTER 5

The Polish Forces

Experiences in the Polish-Soviet War of 1918-1921 still shaped Polish Army organisational and operational doctrine in 1939. Unlike the trench warfare, which characterized the First World War, the Polish-Soviet War was a conflict in which the cavalry's mobility played a decisive role. Poland acknowledged the benefits of mobility but was unwilling to invest heavily in many of the expensive, unproven inventions since then and the mechanisation programme was extremely limited by comparison to that of the Germans. In spite of this some tactical innovations had taken place and Polish cavalry brigades were used as a mobile mounted infantry and had some successes against both German infantry and cavalry.

The Polish concept of national forces considered only two services, the Army and Navy. There was no separate air force; air units formed part of both Army and Navy. The President of the Polish Republic was the nominal commander in chief, but delegated the actual exercise of command to the Inspector General of the Armed Forces and the Minister of War. In peacetime the Inspector General prepared mobilization plans, supervised training, made recommendations on matters pertaining to national defence, and controlled the administrative areas and tactical commands of the Army; in time of war he would become the commander in chief. The Minister of War represented the services in the President's cabinet, more as a representative of the Inspector General than as civilian head of the armed forces, and was responsible for a number of diverse functions, including some personnel matters and industrial mobilization. The Navy was supervised by the Minister of War; its size relegated the naval service to a very subordinate role in the Polish Armed Forces Establishment.

The industrial base to support the Polish Armed Forces was still in the process of expansion and modernization in 1939, with the major mining and industrial complex centring about Cracow in southwestern Poland. In addition to this, another industrial region had grown up in the Lublin-Radom area of south central Poland. The total production of both areas in munitions and other military supplies was still limited, and stockpiles had to be built up throughout the country in peacetime. This worked to the disadvantage of the Poles in that the relatively immobile stocks of ammunition, fuel, and other critical supplies would be vulnerable to capture in war and could not be replaced from current production.

However, there was little doubt of the Polish willingness to fight. The fate of Czechoslovakia had not been forgotten and the traditional Slav resentment of German expansion eastward played its part in strengthening Polish determination to resist. Considerable reliance was placed on the assistance of Britain and France.

Polish Renault FT-17 tanks during military parade.

Between 1936 and 1939, Poland invested heavily in industrialization in the Central Industrial Region. Preparations for a defensive war with Germany were ongoing for many years, but most plans assumed fighting would not begin before 1942. To raise funds for industrial development, Poland sold much of the modern equipment it produced. In 1936, a National Defence Fund was set up to collect funds necessary for strengthening the Polish Armed forces. The Polish Army had approximately a million soldiers, but less than half of them were mobilized by 1 September. Latecomers sustained significant casualties when public transport became targets of the Luftwaffe. The Polish military had fewer armoured forces than the Germans, and these units, dispersed within the infantry, were unable to effectively engage the enemy.

Poland was divided into ten corps areas for purposes of military administration and tactical units were attached to the corps area commands for logistical support. Army and army group headquarters did not exist in peacetime. Instead, the Army maintained three higher headquarters known as inspectorates and commanded by senior general officers, at Torun (Thorn), Wilna, and Lwow (Lemberg). From time to time, e.g. for annual manoeuvres, these inspectorates would be assigned tactical divisions and functions as army headquarters. In time of war, the inspectorates would become army or task force commands. Available records make no mention of tactical corps headquarters in wartime; these presumably would be drawn from the corps area commands.

The peacetime Army was authorized 30 infantry divisions and several small mountain infantry brigades, 14 horse cavalry brigades, one mechanized cavalry brigade, and two air divisions. A number of separate engineer, artillery, and other supporting units also existed, but many were assigned a training rather than tactical mission. The personnel ceiling of this peacetime force was set at 280,000, making it necessary to maintain the divisions and brigades at a much reduced strength. An unusual feature of the Polish Army was the faith it placed in armoured trains In 1939 the Poles operated eleven armoured trains and a further four more improvised trains were hastily constructed during the campaign.

The 30 active divisions were distributed three to each of the 10 corps areas as of early 1939. The divisions were numbered 1 through 30, and were identical save for the 21st and 22nd Divisions, which were classified as mountain divisions and assigned to that part of Poland bordered by the Carpathian Mountains. Only 11 active horse cavalry brigades appear to have been in existence, disposed at the rate of one or more to eight of the ten corps areas.

Polish infantry marching towards the front.

During the inter war years Poland made strenuous efforts to modernize her armed forces including importing military technology from Britain who supplied vehicles in the form of these Vickers tankettes which formed the basis of the Polish TKS which saw action in 1939.

Elements of the mechanized cavalry brigade were assigned to several corps areas. Unlike the numbered infantry divisions, the cavalry brigades were designated by the name of the area in which they had their home stations.

Polish armour

More trust was placed in the effectiveness of Polish infantry and horse cavalry than was justified by later events, however there had been some advances in mechanization. In 1939 the Polish Army used variety of vehicles, foreign and licence build. Those included: 574 TK and TKS tankettes.

These light reconnaissance tanks were tiny vehicles that were built on a chassis designed by the British Vickers company. The Poles also fielded 102 obsolete Renault FT-17 light tanks of Great War vintage. The Polish tank forces were completed by 132 7TP light tanks, 38 Vickers 6-ton light tanks, 53 R-35 light tanks and three Hotchkiss H-35 light tanks. The tanks were supplemented by approximately 100 armoured cars.

The Polish Army's tanks were grouped in Light Tank Battalions (numbered 1st, 2nd and 21st) there were also seven independent Light Tank Companies (12th, 111th, 112th, 113th 121st and 1st and 2nd Warsaw Defence). The Tankettes served with Infantry Divisions, Cavalry Brigades and Independent units (companies and platoons) attached to larger units. In addition, Poland had single Mechanized Brigade (the 10th). In 1939 this formation was commanded by Colonel Stanislaw Maczek the future commander of the 1st Polish Armoured Division. At the time of the Nazi invasion and new Warsaw based Armoured-Motorised Brigade commanded by Colonel Stefan Rowecki was in the process of being formed. It was too late to take part in the campaign though elements did fight and it's commander later gained lasting fame as the first commander to come of the Polish Home Army.

Supporting (army) troops were distributed throughout all ten areas, each of which had 1 medium artillery regiment and one or more separate tank battalions (of a total of 13). Most of the corps areas also had antiaircraft units (from the Polish Army's five regiments and several separate battalions), and engineers (a total of 14 separate battalions). A signal regiment maintained radio contact between Polish Army Headquarters and major commands in the field, and telephone communication outside the divisions and cavalry brigades was maintained by four separate signal battalions.

Poland's universal conscription program, modelled on that of France, had 204,600 conscripts and volunteers in Army service in 1939. The period of active service varied from 1^{1}/2 years for infantry trainees to 22^{1}/2 months for those of the cavalry, artillery, signal troops, and engineers. The average soldier was hardy and willing to learn, but a lack of modern equipment restricted technical training.

The active noncommissioned officers corps of 30,000 was regarded as well qualified despite its lack of training with modern weapons and techniques. The majority of this group were long-term volunteers and thoroughly schooled. The situation with the 16,300 active officers was somewhat more complex. Junior officers were carefully selected and given uniform training, but field and general officers in most cases had acquired their background in the diverse German, Austro-Hungarian, Russian, and other services, and varied widely in their methods and abilities.

As of 1939, 1,500,000 reservists of the classes 1898-1915 (men 24 to 42 years of age) could be called up on mobilization. An additional 560,000 reservists of the 1888-97 period would also be available if necessary, but their age (43 to 52) would restrict the use of these

These light reconnaissance tanks were tiny vehicles that were built on a chassis designed by the British Vickers company.

troops to security duties and work in the rear areas. The peacetime divisions and army troops would be brought to full strength on mobilization, some 15 reserve divisions and supporting units called into service, and the Air Force and Navy expanded.

A National Guard (Obrona Narodowa) also existed, to supplement the active Army and reserve units. The National Guard consisted of men who had completed their training but were without mobilization assignments, men who had not received the prescribed conscript training for one reason or another (including a large number who had been surplus to the draft quotas), and volunteers not yet subject to conscription (21 years of age). The weapons and uniforms issued the National Guard were retained in their homes, and ammunition at the local depots of the active units. Training on a part-time basis was carried on, and units up to brigade level were organized.

The Polish National Guard brigade consisted of two regiments of four battalions each, and a total strength of from 2,500 to 4,000 men. Brigades and regiments were commanded by active officers; most of the other officers were from the reserve. In all, 11 brigades were formed, one in each corps area and a naval brigade in Gdynia. In the event of war the National Guard brigades would come under the control of local military commanders.

The active Polish infantry division had three infantry regiments, an artillery regiment, a reconnaissance battalion, an antiaircraft company, a signal company, and rear trains and services. It was planned that each division would have its own engineer battalion and antitank company. As of 1939, this had progressed only to the point where some divisions had small engineer detachments. Transportation in the infantry division was horse drawn.

The infantry regiments each comprised three battalions, of three rifle companies and one heavy weapons company each, an antitank company, a cannon platoon, signal platoon, engineer platoon, and small replacement and service detachments. The rifle companies each had nine light machine guns (similar to the United States Army's Browning automatic rifle, but classified as a machine gun) and three 46mm mortars of Polish manufacture. The weapons companies had 12 heavy machine guns and two 81mm mortars of French origin. The antitank company had nine 37mm guns, and the cannon platoon had two 75mm field pieces of Russian manufacture. The total strength of the regiment, unless it was assigned to border security duties, was 1,450 officers and men. Regiments assigned a border security mission were increased in strength to 2,350 men.

The artillery regiment had two battalions of 75mm guns of French or Polish manufacture, and one battalion of 100mm howitzers of Czech or Polish origin; most of the fire control equipment was obsolete. The replacement of foreign artillery pieces with Polish-made 105mm and 155mm howitzers was making progress as of 1939 but was still far from complete. The authorized strength of the artillery regiment was 780 officers and men. In many cases, the artillery regiment lacked one or more of its battalions or the

The Polish 7TP light tank in action.

German bombers in the skies over Deblin

battalion one battery. Few except artillery units in border areas had their authorized allocation of transportation.

The cavalry brigade consisted of three or four cavalry regiments, and one squadron each of pack artillery, signal troops, and engineers. Each regiment had four line squadrons armed with rifles, light machine guns, sabers, and lances; a machine gun squadron with 12 heavy machine guns; an antitank platoon with four 37mm guns; and a small remount and replacement detachment. The authorized strength of the brigade varied from 720 officers and men to a total of 875, depending upon the brigade's mission.

The Polish Air Force (Lotnicze Wojskowe) was at a severe disadvantage against the German Luftwaffe. Contrary to popular myth this force was not simply destroyed on the ground early in the campaign, as is commonly believed. The Polish Air Force lacked modern fighter aircraft, but despite the limitations of their machines the Polish its pilots were among the world's best trained. The Poles actually claimed some 140 Luftwaffe aircraft which were shot down by the Poles in aerial combat. Many machines were successfully flown to Rumania and Hungary. The undoubted skill of the polish airmen was demonstrated a year later in the Battle of Britain, in which escaped Polish airmen played a major part.

Overall, the Germans enjoyed numerical and qualitative aircraft superiority. Poland had only about 600 modern aircraft. The Polish Air Force fielded roughly 185 PZL P.11 and some 95 PZL P.7 fighters, 175 PZL.23 Karaś B, 35 Karaś A, and by September, over 100 PZL.37 Łoś were produced. There were also over a thousand obsolete transport, reconnaissance and training aircraft. However, for the September Campaign, only some 70 percent of those aircraft were mobilised. Only 36 PZL.37 Łoś bombers were deployed. All those aircraft were

A Polish bridge lies destroyed in a vain attempt to stall the German advance.

of indigenous Polish design, with the bombers being more modern than fighters, according to the Ludomi Rayski air force expansion plan, which relied on a strong bomber force. The Polish fighters were a generation older than their German counterparts. The Polish PZL P.11 fighter, produced in the early 1930s, was capable of only 365 km/h (approximately 220 mi/h), far less than German bombers; to compensate, the pilots relied on its manoeuvrability and high diving speed.

The two air divisions and their air regiments (six in all) had administrative functions only. The tactical unit was the group (three to six per regiment), with two to four squadrons, each with 10-12 aircraft of similar type. In peacetime the air divisions received technical direction from the Air Department in the Ministry of War. Upon mobilization, the Air Force would be reorganized to provide air support for the ground forces and would operate under the tactical control of the army.

Ten reconnaissance, seven fighter, five fighter-bomber, and six groups of liaison aircraft were in existence in mid-1939. There were also two additional air regiments in the process of activation in eastern Poland. The total number of aircraft was 935, including 350 reconnaissance type, 300 fighters, 150 fighter-bombers, and 135 liaison planes. However, a large number of these were obsolete or obsolescent, and suitable only for training purposes. Total personnel strength of the Army Air Force was 6,300 officers and men.

The Navy

The surface fleet of the Polish Navy in 1939 was built around the four destroyers Blyskawica (Lightning), Grom (Thunderbolt), Wicker (Hurricane), and Burza (Squall). The first two vessels each displaced 2,144 tons; the latter 2, 1,540 tons. The heaviest armament comprised 5.1-inch guns and all four destroyers were based at Gdynia. The submarine force consisted of the Orzel (Eagle), Sep (Vulture), Rys (Lynx), Wilk (Wolf), and Zbih (Wildcat), based at Hela; all five were the long-range type, displacing from 980 tons to 1,473 tons. The shore defences of Gdynia and Hela were manned by Navy personnel. Two naval infantry battalions also existed, one at Gdynia and the other a few miles inland, and two additional battalions were in the process of organization. Air support for the Navy consisted of three reconnaissance squadrons, three fighter squadrons, and two torpedo-bomber squadrons, with a total of 85 aircraft.

The Polish Navy was also responsible for the Vistula River, and for this purpose maintained 16 river gunboats and two reconnaissance squadrons of 10 aircraft each. The total peacetime strength of the Polish Naval Force was approximately 3,100 officers and men.

The Polish Navy was essentially a very a small fleet of destroyers, submarines and smaller support vessels. Most Polish surface units followed Operation Peking, left their home ports on 20th August 1939 and escaped by way of the North Sea to join with the British Royal Navy. Submarine forces remained and participated in Operation Worek, with the goal of engaging and damaging German shipping in the Baltic Sea, but they enjoyed little success. In addition to the military vessels many merchant marine ships escaped to join the British merchant fleet and played a valuable and, often overlooked, part in wartime convoys.

Defence plan and dispositions

The Polish defence plan was based on a study originally prepared in 1938 and revised as the Reich gained additional territories surrounding Poland. According to Plan "Z" from the Polish Zachód for West. The Poles estimated in March 1939 that the Germans would make their main attack from Silesia in the direction of Warsaw. An attack from southern Silesia and Slovakia would secure the right flank of the main German attack force. Meanwhile, other German attacks would be launched from Pomerania and East Prussia, to cut The Corridor and support the main drive on the Polish capital. It was estimated the Germans would be able to mobilize 110-120 divisions in all, of which 70-80, including all five panzer, four light, and four motorized infantry divisions would be available for operations against Poland.

Permanent defensive works already existed along the Narew River, at Torun, about Bydgoszcz (Bromberg) and south to the Warta, west of Lodz (Lodsch), about Czestochowa, and west of Katowice (Kattowitz) and Cracow; some of these fortifications had been built prior to World War I. Additional fortifications were built or in the process of construction at Mlawa and along the approaches from East Prussia, west of Bydgoszcz at the base of The Corridor, west of Poznan (Posen), and along the frontier south to Slovakia. These fortifications, some of them only field type, would be used to form the first Polish line of defence.

The field fortifications constructed were far less formidable than might be expected. In the main, they consisted only of earthen entrenchments; barbed wire obstacles, and tank traps. Their construction was entrusted to local military commanders, with the result that there was little uniformity and the extent of the work depended largely upon the initiative of the individual officers. Moreover, many of the works were delayed until the harvest and were not ready when needed. The blocking of smaller rivers to make possible later flooding was unsuccessful due to the dry weather which held all through the summer.

Orders deploying the Polish Army according to Plan "Z" were issued on 23rd March 1939. The deployment was an obvious attempt to hold the entire country, and probably based on the belief that the intervention of Britain and France in the west would force a number of German divisions to withdraw. The deployment was faulty from a military standpoint, since The Corridor was indefensible and troop units in that area would be in constant danger of encirclement from East Prussia and Pomerania. Polish forces deployed in the Poznan area would be situated in a salient flanked on the north and south by German territory, and units in the Cracow area would be threatened by encirclement from Slovakia and southern Silesia, However, The Corridor and Poznan areas contained a large part of Poland's agricultural resources, and Cracow the country's mines and heavy industry. In addition to these economic aspects, the psychological effect of the surrender of these vital areas without a struggle had to be considered. The Polish defence plan, was shaped by political determination to deploy forces directly at the German-Polish border, based upon London's promise to come to Warsaw's military aid in the event of invasion. Moreover, with the nation's most valuable natural resources, industry and highly populated regions near the western border (Silesia region), Polish policy centred on their protection, especially since many politicians feared that if Poland were to retreat from the regions disputed by Germany (like the Polish Corridor, cause of the famous "Danzig or War" ultimatum), Britain and France would sign a separate peace treaty with Germany similar to the Munich Agreement of 1938. In addition, none of its allies had specifically guaranteed Polish borders or territorial integrity. On those grounds, Poland disregarded French advice to deploy the bulk of their forces behind the natural barriers of the wide Vistula and San rivers, even though some Polish generals supported it as a better strategy. The Zachód plan did allow the Polish armies to retreat inside the country, but it was supposed to be a slow retreat behind prepared positions near the rivers (Narew, Vistula and San), giving the country time to finish its mobilisation, and was to be a slow retreat behind prepared positions near the rivers (Narew, Vistula and San), giving the country time to finish its mobilisation, and was to be turned into a general counteroffensive when the Western Allies launched their own promised offensive.

The Polish Army's most pessimistic fallback plan involved retreat behind the river San to the southeastern voivodships and their lengthy defence (the Romanian bridgehead plan). The British and French estimated that Poland should be able to defend that region for two to three months, while Poland estimated it could hold for at least six months. This Polish plan was based around the expectation that the Western Allies would keep their end of the signed alliance treaty and quickly start an offensive of their own. However, neither the French nor the British government made plans to attack Germany while the Polish campaign was being fought. In addition, they expected the war to develop into trench warfare much like World War I had, forcing the Germans to sign a peace treaty restoring Poland's borders. The Polish government, however, was not notified of this strategy and based all of its defence plans on

A German heavy flak gun in position.

promises of quick relief by their Western allies.

The plan to defend the borders contributed vastly to the Polish defeat. Polish forces were stretched thin on the very long border and, lacking compact defence lines and good defence positions along disadvantageous terrain, mechanized German forces often were able to encircle them. In addition, supply lines, were often poorly protected. Approximately one-third of Poland's forces were concentrated in or near the Polish Corridor (in northwestern Poland), where they were perilously exposed to a double envelopment — from East Prussia and the west combined and isolated in a pocket. In the south, facing the main avenues of a German advance, the Polish forces were thinly spread. At the same time, nearly another one-third of Poland's troops were massed in reserve in the north-central part of the country,

An amphibious crossing organised by German combat engineers.

between the major cities of ‚ódê and Warsaw, under commander in chief Marshal Edward Rydz-Śmigły. The Poles' forward concentration in general forfeited their chance of fighting a series of delaying actions, since their army, unlike some of Germany's, travelled largely on foot and was unable to retreat to their defensive positions in the rear or to man them before they were overrun by German mechanized columns.

Temporary bridges were built along the Vistula and the Warta, to facilitate the movement of reserves to threatened points. Several infantry divisions and smaller units were transferred from their garrison areas in eastern Poland to the central and western parts of the country. A number of individual reservists were called up for service and several reserve divisions mobilized and assigned to defensive missions with the active divisions. National Guard units in The Corridor and Poznan areas were mobilized for frontier defence service.

In the north, a special force of two infantry divisions and two cavalry brigades, under Maj. Gen. C. Mlot-Fijalkowski, was disposed along the Biebrza and Narew Rivers and assigned the mission of holding that part of the Polish frontier north of the Grodno-Warsaw rail line and the frontier with Lithuania (Narew Group). On the left of the Narew Group, a similar force of two infantry divisions and two cavalry brigades, under Brig. Gen. E. Przedzymirski-Krukowicz, was assigned the defence of the Mlawa area and the direct route to Warsaw (Modlin Army). Another force of five infantry divisions and a cavalry brigade (Pomorze Army), under the command of Maj. Gen. W. Bortnowski, held The Corridor to a junction with the command of Maj. Gen. T. Kutrzeba, assigned four infantry divisions and two cavalry brigades for the defence of the Poznan salient (Poznan Army).

Five infantry divisions and two cavalry brigades, under command of Maj. Gen. J. Rommel, held the Lodz area (Lodz Army) and southward to a junction with the force of Brig. Gen. A. Szylling, assigned seven infantry divisions and a cavalry brigade for the defence of the vital Cracow region (Cracow Army). Temporarily, light forces would hold the crossings from Slovakia. The general reserve force, centred about Warsaw and in two concentrations to the northeast and northwest of the capital, consisted of twelve infantry divisions, the mechanized cavalry brigade, and one horse cavalry brigade. These concentrations of the general reserve would counterattack major German penetrations in the direction of Warsaw and provide the force necessary if the Poles were eventually to go over to the offensive. The port area of Gdynia also organized a defence force the strength of a small division by combining the naval infantry force, reservists, and seamen assigned to shore installations.

The ground defensive organization involved most of the active and several reserve (infantry) divisions, all the active cavalry brigades, and the bulk of the naval personnel assigned to shore duties. In addition, the Pomorze, Lodz, and Cracow Armies and the general reserve force were assigned reserve divisions that would be called up on mobilization. Where possible, troops were retained in garrison areas and the units assigned defensive missions. In some cases units had to move to areas better situated for defence. In The Corridor area these moves aroused the resentment of the German part of the population and formed the basis for German charges of war preparations on the part of the Poles.

The Polish commands formed had no standard corps organization and few other units except infantry divisions and cavalry brigades. However, reference is generally made to them as armies, except for the Narew Group, with the name of the geographic area they were assigned to defend.

Some changes were made in the dispositions of these Polish forces during the several months preceding the German attack. The Carpathian Army was formed under Maj. Gen. K. Fabrycy to defend the southern frontier of Poland. The Carpathian Army was allocated only three mountain infantry brigades, but an additional force formed for the general reserve and consisting of one active division and a partially mobilized reserve division was stationed in the area in the immediate rear of Fabrycy's force. The mechanized cavalry brigade was transferred to the Cracow Army, an infantry division of the Lodz Army was transferred to the general reserve, and a provisional tank brigade was organized and attached to the general reserve. This was the force, not fully mobilized, with which Poland was to confront the bulk of Germany's 102 divisions, supported by a total of 3,000 tanks and more than 4,000 aircraft.

CHAPTER 6

German Operational Plans

The German plan for what became known as the September Campaign was devised by General Franz Halder, chief of the general staff, and directed by General Walther von Brauchitsch, the commander in chief of the upcoming campaign. It called for the start of hostilities before a declaration of war, and pursued a doctrine of mass encirclement and destruction of enemy forces. The infantry – far from completely mechanized but fitted with fast moving artillery and logistic support – was to be supported by German tanks and small numbers of truck-mounted infantry these were Schützen regiments, the forerunners of the Panzergrenadiers. Their role was to assist the rapid movement of troops and concentrate on localized parts of the enemy front, eventually isolating segments of the enemy, surrounding, and destroying them. The pre-war armoured idea was not known as Blitzkrieg until an American journalist coined the phrase. In the thirties the possibilities offered by new technology indicated the possibility of an entirely this new system of mechanized warfare which was strongly advocated by some generals, including Heinz Guderian. Their new concept saw armour as the device for punching holes in the enemy's front and ranging deep into rear areas. In practice however, the campaign in Poland would be fought along more traditional lines. This stemmed from conservatism on the part of the German high command, who mainly restricted the role of armour and mechanized forces to supporting the conventional infantry divisions.

April-May 1939

Headquarters OKW began to draft the timetable of preparations for the concentration against Poland immediately following the issue on 3rd April of the second part of the annual armed forces directive. The timetable would form the master schedule for the movements, security measures, and other steps necessary to enable the German forces to launch an attack at the time and in the manner directed by Hitler should the Führer decide to settle his differences with Poland by war. Its completion, however, would have to await the recommendations of the three services, which began their planning and prepared recommendations for the deployment of forces on the basis of the instructions contained in Plan WEISS.

Each service selected one or more major commands to direct operations in the field. Some deviation from the mobilization plan of the Army was found to be necessary in the case of the higher ground commands, as OKH directed the organization of two army group headquarters. The peacetime Heeresgruppenkommomdo 1, under Generaloberst Fedor von Bock, that would normally have become Second Army on mobilization, was designated to form the headquarters of Army Group North. Headquarters OKH also directed the

The Polish cruiser Gryf sinking after a surprise attack

organization of a provisional headquarters under Generaloberst Gerd von Rundstedt, then in retirement at Kassel; this headquarters would become Army Group South, with a staff composed largely of VII Corps personnel who would have been assigned to form Twelfth Army on mobilization. The Luftwaffe selected its First and Fourth Air Forces. The Navy designated Naval Command East (Marinegruppenkommando Ost), the naval equipment of the Heeresgruppenkommando, as the headquarters for fleet units to be committed to the campaign.

A pilot's view of Poland from the air. Note the Polish trenches.

Bock's chief of staff was Generalleutnant Hans von Salmuth and his operations officer was Colonel Wilhelm Haase at the time. The provisional headquarters was to be known as Arbeitsstdb Rundstedt (Working Staff Rundstedt) temporarily. As his chief of staff, Rundstedt was assigned Generalleutnant Fritz Erich von Manstein, commander of an infantry division. Col. Guenther Blumentritt, chief of training at OKH, was to become Rundstedt's operations officer. The provisional headquarters had no peacetime counterpart, and almost all of the Arbeitssbab Rundstedt planning had to be carried on by the three officers originally assigned and by two General Staff officers detailed to the project in the course of the summer. Rundstedt remained much of the time at his home, while Manstein and Blumentritt continued as division commander and OKH staff officer, respectively, working on the plans as an additional duty. Blumentritt's dual position in operational planning and normal training made it possible to camouflage many of the pre-operational movements of troops as part of the annual training and manoeuvre program.

The Army, Navy, and Air Force drew up three separate but coordinated campaign plans. As a point of interest, the Army plan included the commitment of two regiments and several smaller separate units of the SS Verfuegungstruppen, the armed affiliate of the National Socialist Party. The SS military force was still in the process of development, and only four regiments and a few separate small units were in existence in 1939.

Hitler was briefed on the Army's plan on 26th-27th April. The Führer approved the OKH concept of an attack by two army groups, from north and south, destroying the Polish armies in the western part of the country and capturing Warsaw. On the northern front, Fourth Army would cut The Corridor at its base and take Grudziadz (Graudenz). The establishment of contact between the Reich proper and East Prussia by Fourth Army would be followed by a Third Army attack from East Prussia in the direction of Warsaw. On the southern front Rundstedt's army group would advance on Warsaw on a broad front, diverting sufficient forces to hold any Polish attack on its right flank from Galicia and the southeast.

A directive embodying the Army's campaign plan was sent by OKH to Rundstedt and Bock on 1st May for comment and elaboration, and initiated detailed planning by Heeresgruppenkommando 1 and Rundstedt's staff. Both sent appropriate orders to the peacetime commands that would form their army headquarters to initiate planning at the next lower level. As the recommendations of these headquarters were received, they were incorporated into the plans of Rundstedt and Heeresgruppenkommando 1. Bock and Rundstedt submitted their comments and recommendations to OKH late in May.

One attempt was made about this time to discourage Hitler from precipitating a major war by a rash move. As his OKW planners viewed the situation, a war involving the British and French and other western powers could end only in disaster. Therefore, members of the planning staff proposed a war game to consider all features of Germany's strategic situation. Keitel transmitted the request to the Führer, and was refused on the grounds that security and diplomatic negotiations might be endangered. Hitler was firmly convinced that there would be no war with the west over Poland. Meanwhile, OKH revised its campaign plan and OKL and OKM continued with their own planning work.

The OKH Operation Order of 15th June 1939

The first OKH operation order directed Bock's and Rundstedt's headquarters to pursue their planning under their original designations as Heeresgruppenkommando 1 and Arheitsstab Rundstedt. The target date by which the two headquarters were to have worked out all details

German watch a flight of Stukas embarking on yet another mission.

on coordination with the Air Force (and with the Navy, in the case of Army Group North) was set for 20th July. Both army groups had attached to them the commands of the active Army that would form army headquarters on mobilization, and the corps, divisions, and supporting troops considered necessary to accomplish their missions. Direct communication with subordinate headquarters was authorized for planning purposes. Orders directing specific preparations could also be issued by the two headquarters scheduled to become army groups, cutting across normal administrative channels. The movement of troops to the frontier areas would be directed by OKH.

The plan of campaign was expressed in detail, adhering to the general concept of operations, with two army groups attacking from north and south in the direction of the Polish capital. The operation order added one change in directing Third Army to attack simultaneously with Fourth Army and send a strong force to assist Fourth Army in seizing crossings on the Vistula. The major force of Third Army, meanwhile, would attack in the direction of Warsaw without waiting for Fourth Army to establish land contact between the Reich proper and East Prussia. The Polish Army would be destroyed in the western part of Poland, and reserves would be prevented from mobilizing or concentrating to resist the German advance.

This plan of attack, with the German striking power on the north and south, would leave the German center open to Polish counterblows.

Frontier guard units and some reservists would take up defensive positions east of the Oder River at Frankfurt-am-Oder, securing the vital river crossings into the interior of Germany. Local attacks would be launched by these frontier guards and reservists to deceive the Poles and tie down Polish units that might otherwise be moved to oppose the drives of

German soldiers destroying a Polish border barrier.

The command version of the Panzer I.

the northern and southern army groups.

Army Group North was to control the Third and Fourth Armies, under command of General der Artillerie Georg von Kuechler and General der Artillerie Guenther von Kluge. The headquarters for Third Army would be formed from Kuechler's I Corps in East Prussia; the Fourth Army, from Kluge's Group Command 6. While Third Army commenced operations from East Prussia, Fourth Army would make its attack from North Germany's Pomerania.

Third Army would be composed of eight infantry divisions, a Panzer brigade, and a cavalry brigade. Fourth Army would comprise four standard infantry divisions, two motorized infantry divisions, and a Panzer division. Two infantry divisions would be the army group reserve. Army Group North would thus include 14 standard infantry divisions, two motorized infantry divisions, a Panzer division, a Panzer brigade, and a cavalry brigade, together with army group, army, and corps troops.

The attack in the direction of Warsaw would form Third Army's major effort. The force of Third Army that would attack to the southwest and assist Fourth Army in securing crossings along the Vistula would be smaller. Fourth Army would attack to the east and south, cutting off the Polish forces in the northern part of The Corridor and securing the communication and transportation lines between Germany proper and East Prussia. The force of Third Army that attacked to the southwest and the Fourth Army would join in the attack toward Warsaw when their mission in The Corridor area was completed. The capture of Danzig would be accomplished by German reservists already in the city.

Army Group South, the stronger of the two major German ground forces, would include the Eighth, Tenth, and Fourteenth Armies, under General der Infanterie Johannes

The Kreigsmarine launch a mine into the waters of the Baltic.

Blaskowitz, General der Artillerie Walther von Reichenau, and Generaloberst Wilhelm List, in that order. Eighth Army would be formed from Blaskowitz's Group Command 3; Tenth Army, from Reichenau's Group Command 4; Fourteenth Army, from List's Group Command 5. The Eighth and Tenth Armies would attack from northern Silesia; Fourteenth Army, from southern Silesia and the satellite state of Slovakia.

Eighth Army would comprise four infantry divisions. Tenth Army would be composed of six infantry, two motorized infantry, two Panzer, and three light divisions. Fourteenth Army would include five infantry, one light, and two Panzer divisions. Three mountain and 6 infantry divisions would be the army group reserve. Army Group South thus would have 21 infantry, four Panzer, two motorized infantry, four light, and three mountain divisions.

The main effort would be made by Tenth Army, strongest of the three, striking toward Warsaw. Eighth Army would move on Lodz and secure the left (north) flank of Tenth Army against strong Polish forces known to be in the Poznan-Kutno area and capable of interfering with Tenth Army's mission. The situation as it developed in the area of Army Group South would determine the further employment of Eighth Army. On the right (southeast) flank of Army Group South, Fourteenth Army would take Cracow and push to the east to protect the right flank of Tenth Army from attack by Polish forces moving into western Galicia from Lwow and the east. The junction of Army Group North and Tenth Army at Warsaw would seal off Polish units in western Poland and prevent their escape to the area east of the Narew-Vistula-San River line.

The future army group commanders held several dissenting opinions concerning the OKH plan. Rundstedt believed that Tenth Army should move first to destroy the Polish forces on its front, diverting some units if necessary from the drive on Warsaw. This was resolved when Rundstedt was ordered to move directly on the Polish capital] with the Tenth Army. Rundstedt also desired more cavalry to screen his left flank. Accordingly, OKH allocated the motorized SS Regiment Adolf Hitler to the Eighth Army. For his part, Bock questioned the advisability of a heavy attack on Warsaw from the west. Instead he favoured strengthening Third Army at the expense of Fourth Army, once The Corridor had been cut, and executing a deep drive east of the Polish capital to prevent the escape of Polish forces into the vast Pripyat Marches. Smaller German forces could be used to tie down the Poles west of Warsaw, but the major effort would be in the east. Bock was granted some additional latitude in directing his campaign, but his major objection to the OKH concept was not resolved until operations were under way.

Troop movements to begin the implementation of the OKH plan would be carried out in three series. The first of these would involve the movement of a number of infantry divisions and supporting units to Germany's eastern frontier area and to East Prussia. Manoeuvres had been scheduled, including armoured exercises in central Germany, and the Reich had announced the intention of strengthening its eastern frontiers, so the first troop movements would not necessarily appear as a hostile gesture toward Poland. Troops from the Reich were also scheduled to participate in the Tannenberg Memorial ceremonies in East Prussia in August, to commemorate the victory of Hindenburg's Eighth Army over the Russian Narew Army in the Allenstein area in August 1914. The second and third series of movements would involve the headquarters staffs and their supporting troops; the armoured, light, and motorized infantry divisions; and the remaining elements of the infantry divisions. The day all preparations would be completed for the attack was designated as Y-day. Final preparations were to be scheduled as Y-3, Y-2, etc., as soon as Hitler specified the exact date for Y-day.

The OKW timetable

The timetable of preparations was issued to the Army, Navy, and Air Force on 14th July and scheduled the movement of forces as recommended by the services to enable them to execute their attack plans. The movement of some Army units for the purpose of working on the Ostwall, or eastern counterpart of the Westwall, had already begun, so the timetable contained the schedule for the remainder of the movements in the first series of troop shifts. Notations in

One of the first actions of the war was the attack on the Polish Post office which was supported by this armoured car of the SS Hiemwehr Danzig.

Surviving Polish defenders are escorted away from the scene of the fighting in the aftermath of the battle. These men were later tortured, tried and executed.

the timetable called for decisions by Hitler prior to the undertaking of successive major steps planned, thereby enabling the Führer to exercise close control over the entire undertaking. The timetable itself did not constitute an order. Rather, it provided only a schedule, and orders for movements or measures to be taken had to be given by OKW or the service directly concerned. Where political or diplomatic considerations were involved, OKW reserved decision or gave specific authorization to one of the services to order appropriate action. Orders to various departments of the Reich government, as the transportation and postal services, were also to be given by OKW.

In addition to the movement of active units to the east, the timetable provided for the mobilization of a number of reservists for the Army and Air Force prior to the attack. A total of 386,000 Army and 55,000 Luftwaffe reservists would be ordered to report for active duty, ostensibly for manoeuvres.

The timetable provided for securing the Führer's decision regarding Y-Day by 23rd August. With this decision, the "Y" or final movement would be ordered, and units in concentration areas would begin their moves to assembly areas for the attack. On Y-1, Hitler's order for the attack was to be given by 12:00, after which the "X" mobilization would be directed (calling up the reserve divisions without public proclamation), and the code word setting the precise time for the attack was to be communicated to the headquarters of the three services.

Hitler's order of Y-1 setting the exact time for the attack was to be followed by the implementation of Plan WEST. The first westward movement would involve seven active divisions, several of which were already training in the western frontier area. The frontier commands were to be absorbed into the First, Fifth, and Seventh Armies, and Army Group C would be assigned responsibility for the defence of the Westwall.

Logistical support

The Reichsbahn (German Federal Railways) would transport the bulk of the troops and their equipment to the frontier area. Movements to mid-August, carefully scheduled, required no mobilization of the German railroad system. As of 16th August, however, there was to be a curtailment of traffic and as many special trains as possible (excursions, etc.) would be cancelled. On 18th August precautions were to be taken to safeguard rail lines and installations.

On Y-2 the Reichsbahn would make the necessary arrangements preliminary to its mobilization. On Y-1 the security of rail lines and installations was to be strengthened by additional railway police and the Reichsbahn, with the rest of the German transportation system, would go on a wartime basis. Foreign rail traffic in Germany was to be kept under observation and preparations made to halt it if necessary.

The Autobahn highway system was to be inspected effective 17th August. Stops for motor columns would be kept available, and obstructions to traffic repaired immediately. On Y-l the special telephone system of the Autobahn was to be tied in with the rest of the German telephone communications system. The trucks and other motor vehicles necessary for military use would be requisitioned from government agencies, industry, and private owners.

The Reichspost (German Postal Service), which controlled the telephone and telegraph systems as well as the mails, held available special lines for long-distance military traffic even in peacetime. On Y-2 all telephone and telegraph installations would be secured. On Y-1 the special nets for military traffic were to be opened. Regular telephone and telegraph traffic would be kept to the minimum, and communications traffic to foreign countries was to be monitored or held up. All telephone and telegraph communications to Poland and Lithuania were to be cut off at midnight of the day preceding Y-day.

Enormous stocks of rations, ammunition, gasoline, spare parts for a wide range of vehicle types, bridging equipment, and hay and forage for the animals of the infantry and mountain divisions were to be made available. Provisions would also have to be made for moving depots forward as the units advanced. It was estimated the fuel problem would be particularly acute with the armoured columns, moving through a primarily agricultural country.

The food supplies required by the troops prior to the attack would be provided by the local Wehrkreise. Eighth and Tenth Armies were to be supplied with rations by Wehrkreis VIII, with headquarters in Breslau. Fourteenth Army would draw upon Wehrkreis XVII, in Vienna. Third Army was to be supplied by Wehrkreis I, in Koenigsberg (East Prussia), and

The logistical back up for the German army was still largely horse-drawn.

The devasted forest of the Westerplatte following the bombardment of the Schleswig Holstein.

Fourth Army by Wehrkreis II, at Stettin (Pomerania).

Rations for the troops were to be secured in advance of operations from the Wehrkreise and stored in depots by each army. According to German practice, the divisions, corps, and army troop units would draw directly on these depots. Initial stocks were to consist of a ten day supply of field rations and one emergency ration. A ten day supply of oats and sufficient hay for the animals for two days would be stored in the same depot and issued with the rations. A notation in the OKH field order that biscuits would be provided in place of bread for the last three days of the ten day period, since the issue bread would remain fresh for approximately one week only, may perhaps serve as an example for the completeness of preparations. Should further rations, hay, and forage not be available for issue after the start of operations, e.g. if the units overextended their supply lines or army ration installations were unable to maintain the rate of advance of the combat units, the divisions might permit local requisitioning down to battalion.

A total of four times the basic load of ammunition (a specified amount to be carried by the troops or in unit transportation) was to be made available. One load would be carried by individuals (pistol, rifle, and submachine gun ammunition) and in the trucks, wagons, and trains of the unit (machine gun, mortar, and artillery ammunition). A second load would be available for issue from the army ammunition depot, and two more loads would be stored on rail sidings and moved forward as the situation necessitated. Every rifleman required 90 rounds, every light machine gun 3,750 rounds, and every division artillery piece 300 rounds, for each of the four loads. Third Army, drawing on depots in East Prussia and separated from the Reich, was to have a total of six loads available, and would store four extra loads for those Fourth Army units Bock planned to move to East Prussia once a junction was effected across the Polish Corridor.

Gasoline and oil sufficient to drive each vehicle a total of 750 kilometers (approximately 450 miles) under normal operating conditions was to be provided units in assembly areas. All gasoline tanks were to be filled and the surplus carried in cans on each vehicle, on unit supply trucks, or in the regimental and division trains. Stocks equal to this initial issue of fuel were to be kept in tank cars along the rail lines, ready to move ahead for issue as the units advanced. Army Group South, with its heavy concentration of armoured vehicles, was to have an additional allocation of 1,500 tons of fuel, to be held on trucks in the vicinity of Breslau and ready to move on short notice to units where it was needed.

The various armies were to draw replacement vehicles, tires, and spare parts from specified motor pools and tire depots in the Zone of the Interior. Major repairs would also be affected by the repair shops of these motor pools. In the Army Group North area, Third Army would use the motor pool in Koenigsberg and Fourth Army that in Stettin. In the Army Group South area, Eighth Army would use the motor pool in Breslau, Tenth Army the motor pools in Breslau and Oppeln, and Fourteenth Army the motor pool in Vienna. The tire depots, for the most part, were in the general vicinity of the motor pools or in nearby cities. All motor pools and their supply warehouses were to receive special issues of spare parts by 20th August.

It was presumed that the Poles would destroy a large number of bridges, particularly those across the Vistula and the broader rivers. Rail lines and terminal installations might

German field artillery awaits the order to fire.

also be damaged by bombing, artillery fire, or demolitions. Many of the Polish roads would not stand up well under sustained pounding by trucks, the artillery's prime movers, and tanks. In anticipation of these contingencies, bridging equipment was to be stored in each army group area, and a number of engineer bridging units attached to each army group and army. In addition to the bridging units, each army group and army was to receive road building, general service, and construction engineer battalions. Special engineer staffs would be attached to the army groups and armies to provide technical direction for all engineer work within the army group and army areas. Railway engineer personnel would be available for putting captured rail lines back into operation.

Sick and wounded personnel requiring hospitalization would be sent to available garrison or civilian hospitals, pending the organization of general hospitals in the army rear areas. Veterinarians were to use civilian facilities whenever military installations for the care of sick and injured animals were not available, until such time as veterinary service in the army rear areas could be established.

Temporary executive power (vollziehende Gewalt, a form of martial law) in designated areas of Silesia would be granted to the commander of Army Group South, and in portions of Moravia and Slovakia to the commander of Fourteenth Army. Since the two armies of Army Group North would be operating from either side of the Polish Corridor, the Commanders of each were to be granted temporary executive power over designated areas of Reich territory. The time such authority should take effect would in each case be directed by OKH. With this authority, the respective army group and army commanders, in the event of emergency, could utilize civilian manpower and installations, and control the police and local public officials. This authority was to devolve upon the army commanders once the German forces crossed the border into Poland.

In this rough terrain, even horses were frequently tested to their limits.

A German JU52 transport plane in the skies above Poland.

Arrangements were also to be made for evacuation of prisoners taken. In the Army Group North area, Fourth Army's captives would be evacuated to a central collecting point at Stargard; Third Army's would go to collecting points to be set up by Wehrkreis I. In the area of Army Group South, prisoners of war taken by Eighth and Tenth Armies would be evacuated to collecting points in Silesia. Fourteenth Army would erect such detention centers in Slovakia as it deemed necessary. With the exception of those sent to Slovakia, all prisoners of war would come under the control of the Replacement and Training Army (Ersatzheer) upon arrival at the collecting point. The collecting points themselves were not considered as camps for final disposition, but rather as temporary holding points pending further evacuation or exchange.

Radio silence was to be observed by all units in their concentration and assembly areas, but normal traffic of garrison troops maintained to avoid arousing the suspicions of the Poles. Land cables and telephone lines for use by the incoming headquarters staffs were to be installed by garrison troops and special signal personnel. These advance preparations could be made only within the Reich, however. Those units of Fourteenth Army that would concentrate in Slovakia would be moving into an area not occupied by German garrison troops and any overt activity would be certain to draw the attention of the residents of the region and quite possibly their Polish neighbours. Thus Fourteenth Army was to plan lines to be installed hastily when the units to concentrate in Slovakia moved into their assembly areas. Special signal troops would be assigned the army groups to put captured Polish signal installations and facilities back into operation as the attack progressed.

The APO number system would go into effect with the arrival of troops in concentration areas. No mail was to be delivered or collected for a period of five days following the start of operations.

The Navy and Air Force

The role of the Navy in the Polish Campaign was outlined in Admiral Raeder's annual directive on 16th May. Naval units would participate in operations to the extent of destroying or capturing the small Polish naval and merchant fleets, keeping clear the sea lanes to East Prussia, blockading Danzig and Gdynia, bombarding Polish shore installations, and rendering Army Group North such assistance as it might require in the course of its operations. Marinegruppe Ost, under command of Generaladmiral Conrad Albrecht, would control three cruisers, two flotillas of destroyers (eight or more ships), 14 submarines, and a number of torpedo boats and other light craft. These naval units were to be so deployed in the Baltic area so as to be able to reach their assigned battle stations before hostilities were begun. The naval units assigned to missions against Poland were assured of a 48-hour advance-warning period to reach these assigned stations. The bulk of the fleet, including most of the operational U-boats, would take up battle stations in the North Sea and the Atlantic, ready to engage the British and French in the event of Allied intervention.

An operation order was issued on 21st August by Naval Command East, giving the latest estimates of Polish naval strength and assigning specific missions to units designated to participate in the attack on Poland. The training ship (formerly battleship) Schleswig-Holstein was to be sent on a visit to Danzig shortly before the outbreak of hostilities, and was to anchor in the harbor there; its mission was the bombardment of Polish shore installations. Other surface units would proceed out of sight of land to Gdynia and Hela (a Polish fort on the Hela Peninsula in the Bay of Danzig) and destroy their coastal batteries.

Fire was to be opened on Hela at H-hour and on Gdynia one hour later, to prevent losses to German aircraft scheduled to make a feint attack at first light to cover the approach of the surface craft. Neutral ships would be given 10 hours to clear the ports, after which both Danzig and Gdynia were to be blockaded by mines, surface craft, and submarines. The property of neutrals was to be scrupulously respected to prevent incidents, and German warships would not enter neutral waters. Special care was to be taken to avoid damage to the city of Danzig. The Navy would be instructed to commence hostilities by a system of code words and numbers disguised as radio traffic of the merchant marine.

Luftwaffe issued its first directive for operations against Poland in mid-May. The First and Fourth Air Forces, designated to direct the air effort, were commanded at that time by General der Flieger Albert Kesselring and General der Flieger Alexander Loehr, respectively. The First Air Force would operate in the area of Army Group North and give close support to the Third and Fourth Armies. The Fourth Air Force was to operate in the area of Army Group South and support the Eighth, Tenth, and Fourteenth Armies. Air force planning proceeded in much the same manner as planning by the Army.

As major subordinate headquarters, the First Air Force would control the 1st Air Division, commanded by General lieutenant Ulrich Grauert, operating from bases in Pomerania, and the Luftwaffe Training Division (consisting of picked squadrons formerly assigned to experimental work), commanded by Generalleutnant Helmuth Foerster, operating from bases in East Prussia. For its major subordinate headquarters, the Fourth Air

Taking down the Polish national emblem in Danzig.

German pioneers quickly replaced the bridges blown down by the Poles.

Force was to control the 2nd Air Division, under Generalleutnant Bruno Loerzer, with headquarters 25 miles southeast of Breslau in German Silesia, and a provisional command known as the Richthofen Air Division. (The German term for General major Wolfgang Freiherr von Richthofen's position was Fliegerführer z. b. V., or Air Commander for Special Employment, and his force consisted of approximately one air division.) The Richthofen Air Division was to establish its headquarters approximately 70 miles southeast of Breslau, enabling the division to support Fourteenth Army.

The OKL reserve was to consist of the 7th Air Division at Liegnitz in Silesia. The 7th Air Division included the 1st Parachute Infantry Regiment and several air transport groups. (Parachute troops were part of the Luftwaffe under the German concept of organization. Goering had forced this arrangement for paratroop units and antiaircraft units already formed by the Army at the time the armed forces had been expanded.)

The two air forces assigned to direct the air effort against Poland would control 36 groups and approximately 1,400 offensively armed aircraft. All of the Luftwaffe's dive bomber force, 70 percent of its bombers, and 50 percent of the fighter force would be committed to operations, and the two air forces deployed to meet an attack in the west would be weakened by the diversion of combat units to the air effort in the east.

The Air Force plan of operations gave first priority to the destruction of the Polish Air Force in the air and on the ground. The 12 major Polish air bases and 75 smaller airfields and landing strips were known to the Luftwaffe, and the first few days should suffice to eliminate any Polish threat from the skies. The German Air Force would then be able to turn its attention to bombing and strafing Polish columns moving to the front, and bombing marshalling yards and rear areas where Polish reserves would be gathering.

To maintain close contact with Army units it was to support, the Air Force detailed liaison officers to the major ground commands. A Luftwaffe commander for all air reconnaissance and flak units supporting the Army was also detailed to each of the two army group headquarters.

The concentration of forces

The first troop movements to the east, from late June to mid-August, involved a number of infantry divisions, some of the corps headquarters, and many of the service units required to establish communications and supply installations that would be needed by the troops to follow. The first movement occurred between 26th June and 15th July, when four infantry divisions were dispatched to Pomerania and Silesia. Five more infantry divisions followed between 15th July and 4th August. In some cases troop units dispatched to the frontier areas were rotated back to their home stations once again before their final move to concentration areas shortly before the attack. This measure helped allay Polish fears about an imminent invasion.

An infantry division and panzer brigade arrived in East Prussia during the first week of August. A possible Polish attack against East Prussia in the event of hostilities made it essential that this easternmost German area be secured while troops were concentrating in Pomerania and Silesia. Part IV of the annual military directive provided for the organization of Third Army by I Corps in East Prussia in the event of mobilization. Unlike the other army headquarters that would be formed from existing group commands and corps, Third Army

This Polish armoured train was destroyed by a dive bombing attack.

German panzers approaching the Brda River.

in peacetime had a small permanent staff and could organize rapidly for defence. The exposed province of East Prussia, surrounded on its land sides by Poland and Lithuania, made necessary such preparation for a quick transition from a peace to a war footing.

The concluding movements in the first phase of deployment eastward were completed in early August. A signal regiment arrived in Pomerania to set up the communications net for Army Group North headquarters, and a corps headquarters and two infantry divisions arrived in the Fourth Army area. A corps headquarters, engineers and military police, and an infantry division moved into Eighth Army's area. A corps headquarters, a signal regiment, construction engineers, and two infantry divisions moved into the Tenth Army's area. Two corps headquarters, a signal regiment, and three infantry divisions moved into the area of the Fourteenth Army. A signal regiment and military police units also arrived as the forward echelon of Army Group South's army group troops.

The second series of transfers was designated as the "A" movement, and set in motion in mid-August with Hitler's decision to continue with the build-up of forces. In the north, the personnel assigned to form the army group staff moved to Bad Polzin and established headquarters. Personnel to form Fourth Army established headquarters at Jastrow. Units scheduled to become army group and army troops and moved in at the same time included engineers, signal units, artillery, and air units directly attached to the ground forces for observation and courier purposes. On 16th August four reserve divisions composed of personnel resident in East Prussia were called up for training. A corps headquarters, a panzer division, and elements of two motorized divisions were shifted into the Fourth Army area.

In the south, the headquarters of Rundstedt's army group was established at Neisse.

Eighth Army headquarters assembled at Breslau, Tenth Army at Oppeln, and Fourteenth Army headquarters at Neutitschein. All of these headquarters, as well as those of the army group and armies in the north, would become operational on OKH order. The corps headquarters and divisions deployed in the "A" movement to the Army Group South area included elements of three Tenth Army corps, with two Panzer, two motorized infantry, and three light divisions. One corps headquarters moved into Fourteenth Army's area.

The "Y" movement followed immediately upon the "A" movement and was set in motion with Hitler's decision of 23rd August setting 26 August as Y-day, when all preparations were to be complete. The remaining elements of the divisions and corps which redeployed only part of their forces in the "A" movement were brought up, together with army group, army, and corps troops, and additional corps, divisions, and separate units were moved in. The remaining elements of two divisions closed into the Fourth Army area in the north. In the south, the remainder of three corps and their divisions moved into Tenth Army assembly areas; one light and two panzer divisions arrived in the area of the Fourteenth Army. For security purposes, a number of the armoured and motorized units moved in organic transportation by night from manoeuvre areas in central Germany.

Concurrent naval movements from mid-August brought fleet units and attached air elements within striking range of Poland or into position to counter British and French attempts at intervention. On 19th August 14 long-range submarines left their home bases at Wilhelmshaven Kiel for Atlantic war stations and the British Isles area. The Graf Spee departed on 21st August to rendezvous with the supply ship Altmark, and take up position as a commerce raider in the South Atlantic. Two more submarines left for the Atlantic area on 22nd and 23rd August.

Naval Command West (Marinegruppe West) was organized on 23rd August to control fleet units sent on interception missions against the British and French. The Deutschland left Wilhelmshaven for a rendezvous with the supply ship Westenwald, and the mission of raiding Allied commerce in the North Atlantic. The Scharnhorst and Gneisenau took up positions in the North Sea. The Admiral Scheer, the cruisers Hipper and Leipzig, three divisions of destroyers (six or more ships), 24 of the smaller submarines, approximately 100 naval aircraft, and a number of light vessels for patrol purposes, minesweeping, and local defence missions completed the naval units assigned to meet any Allied attack from the west.

Naval Command East was assigned the Nuernberg as flagship for the direction of operations against the Polish Navy, merchant marine, and port defences. The cruisers, two flotillas of destroyers, 14 submarines, and other naval vessels and aircraft to be committed against Poland were in the Baltic area and prepared for active operations on short notice.

The First Air Force headquarters moved to East Prussia and the Fourth to Breslau. The First Air Force comprised 800 aircraft, including 500 bombers, 180 dive-bombers, and 120 fighters. The Fourth Air Force controlled 590 aircraft, including 310 bombers, 160 dive-bombers, and 120 fighters. The bomber aircraft were mostly Messerschmitt 111s and Dornier 17s. The dive-bombers were Junkers 87s, more popularly known as Stukas. The fighters were mostly Messerschmitt 109s and 110s. The OKL reserve had a few additional bombers and two air groups with approximately 250 Junkers 52 transports for paratroop operations.

Air units unable to mount their first strikes against Poland from home bases because of range moved to permanent air bases in eastern Germany first, then to landing strips in the vicinity of the frontier on Y-1.

The codeword Befehlsuebernahms ("assume command") was sent out by OKH upon Hitler's decision setting Y-day, and Army Groups North and South and Army Group C and their armies became operational on the 23rd. Naval and air force headquarters designated to participate also become operational at the same time as the army commands.

With the build-up of forces complete Hitler set dawn on Y-day, 26th August, as the time for the attack, knowing the Russians would not intervene. As General Halder noted in his diary, there would be no further orders—everything would proceed according to plan. The divisions and other units moved to their final concentration areas as scheduled.

Within the Keich Zone of the Interior, the remaining second, third, and fourth-wave divisions were mobilized. A number of Luftwaffe reserve units were also called up for service. No reinforcement was considered necessary for the Navy, which would mobilize only if Britain and France entered the war.

The period of indecision

Hitler rescinded his order to attack late on 25th August when the British and French refused his overtures and Chamberlain guaranteed support to the Poles. Some German units were already moving toward their final assembly areas, and officer messengers, and in some cases commanders themselves, had to intercept the attack forces personally and relay the order to halt the opening of hostilities. In a few cases small German units crossed the frontier and engaged in clashes with Polish border guards before they could be recalled. Apparently, these skirmishes were considered only an additional provocation by the Poles and part of the German war of nerves.

While the Polish and German forces waited under arms, both reported numerous violations of the frontier and occasional shootings, although none was sufficiently sharp to precipitate hostilities. The Germans still hoped to achieve another bloodless conquest; the Poles thought the firm attitude of the Allies would discourage Hitler from starting what must surely develop into a general war.

The delay in the attack allowed sufficient time for the 10th Panzer Division, just formed in the Protectorate, to move into the area of Fourth Army. (There were no Panzer divisions 6 through 9 at this time. These numbers were to be assigned to the Panzer divisions to be formed from the four light divisions.)

The Navy dispatched two more submarines to Atlantic stations. On 30th August OKM received a report from a radio intercept unit that the Polish destroyers Grom, Blyzkawica, and Burza had left Gdynia. The Polish vessels were kept under observation until it was apparent that they were enroute to the British Isles area. Orders were then issued transferring the cruisers, three of the destroyers, and a number of torpedo boats of the Naval Command East force to Naval Command West. Orders already issued for the mining of the Gdynia Bay area were cancelled. The striking units of Naval Command East would be reduced to the Schleswig-Holstein, a few destroyers, 14 submarines, a number of smaller surface craft, and

Soviet forces pass a unit of German motorcyclists.

attached Luftwaffe units.

Meanwhile, Hitler had regained his determination. Warning orders to the Army, Navy, and Air Force on 30th August instructed the participating headquarters of all three services to prepare for operations on 1 September. In the course of the afternoon of 31st August, they were directed to proceed with the attack: the time for the commencement of hostilities was set for 0445.

As of 31st August the German ground force arrayed against Poland comprised a total of 55 divisions; its composition and dispositions varied in a number of details from the original plan of operations. Plan WEISS had provided for the commitment only of active units to the initial attack; a number of reserve corps and divisions had been added by the mobilization that had proceeded after Hitler postponed the time of attack on 25th August. Several new organizations formed over the preceding few months were also ready for operations, and a number of provisional commands had been formed.

A provisional corps, called Wodrig after its commander, had been created in Third Army control to control two divisions moving south on Warsaw from East Prussia. The XXI Corps, a Wave II command, had also been added to Third Army. The XIX Corps, an active command formed in the course of the summer, was under General der Panzertruppen Heinz Guderian, former chief of Mobile Troops, and would control the Panzer and motorized infantry divisions of Fourth Army. (As the XIV, XV, and XVI Corps, it had no corresponding Wehrkreis organization.) The Panzer brigade sent to East Prussia had been raised to the status of a provisional division and would be committed to operations as Panzer Division Kempf. The 10th Panzer Division had been added to Army Group North. The Kuestrin Frontier Command had been redesignated the 50th Infantry Division. No major changes

Walther von Brauchitsch, architect of the victory, and Adolf Hitler in Warsaw, September 1939.

were made in the order of battle or dispositions of Army Group South but a Wave II corps and several divisions on the right flank of Fourteenth Army would be able to complete their concentration and enter the campaign sooner than would have been the case had operations commenced on 26th August as scheduled.

The frontier commands were also to play a more important part in operations than had first been planned. The three frontier commands along the Westwall were a part of the active Army, but those in the east were police forces under the Reich Ministry of the Interior in peacetime and came under Army control for security duties in the event of war. For the campaign against Poland, the frontier commands in several cases would fill a combat role.

On its extreme left Third Army in East Prussia assigned a small provisional corps of limited combat potential to secure the frontier with Lithuania and the exposed salient of German territory extending into Poland in the direction of Grodno. This force, named Brand, had only two brigades of border and local defence troops. On the Third Army right XXI Corps would cross the frontier with two infantry divisions in a southwesterly direction, with the immediate task of establishing contact with the Fourth Army near Grudziadz. In the center of the Third Army line the I Corps and Corps Wodrig were to attack with one Panzer and four infantry divisions in a drive south toward Warsaw. The 1st Cavalry Brigade was to secure the left flank of the force moving on the Polish capital. One infantry division would form the army reserve. Troops of the XI Frontier Command would be available to hold the rear areas and gaps between Army units as the front moved forward. Third Army would also control the force at Danzig, designated as the Eberhard Brigade and assigned the capture of the city from within.

Fourth Army in Pomerania had the preponderance of armoured and motorized troops in Army Group North. Opposite Gdynia and Danzig, the 1st Frontier Command would sever the upper part of The Corridor. South of the 1st Frontier Command, the XIX Corps, with its one Panzer and two motorized divisions, was to form the major striking force of Fourth Army and cut The Corridor at its base. To the right of the XIX Corps, II Corps would commit two infantry divisions. The III Corps would control one infantry division and a provisional brigade to the south of II Corps. The II and XII Frontier Commands, the latter holding the heavily fortified region east of the junction of the Wartha and Oder Rivers, would complete the Fourth Army front to a junction with Rundstedt's Army Group South. Two infantry divisions would form the army reserve, disposed behind the center of the Fourth Army line.

Army Group North reserves would comprise one infantry division in East Prussia, and one Panzer and two infantry divisions in Pomerania. The division in East Prussia was concentrated in the area immediately adjacent to the junction of the Lithuanian, Polish, and German frontiers. The divisions in Pomerania were concentrated behind the center and right of the Fourth Army line.

On the left, Eighth Army, the smallest of the three armies of Army Group South, would have on its right XIII Corps with two infantry divisions. The X Corps with two infantry divisions would be committed in the center of the army front. The XIII Frontier Command would be disposed to the left of X Corps and extend the army group front northward to a junction with the XII Frontier Command of Brock's Army Group North. Eighth Army would have no divisions its own in reserve, but an infantry division of the army group reserve would be disposed in its area.

Tenth Army would attack in the center of Army Group South. On the right XV Corps would commit one light division. In the right center IV Corps would have two infantry divisions. The XVI Corps, consisting of two Panzer and two infantry divisions would be committed north of the IV Corps. The XI Corps would be on the left of the Tenth Army front with two infantry divisions. The XIV Corps, with two motorized infantry divisions, and two light divisions would form the army reserve. The XIV Corps was disposed on the army north flank, one light division was located behind the XI Corps, and one light division to the rear of the junction of the IV and XV Corps.

On the right of Army Group South, Fourteenth Army would commit the XVIII Corps, made up of one mountain, one light, and one Panzer division. Several Slovak battalions would supplement German reconnaissance units on the extreme right flank and capture a number of villages in Poland that the Slovaks claimed as their own. The XVII Corps would form the center of the Fourteenth Army line with its three infantry divisions. The left of the Fourteenth Army would be held by the VIII Corps, with one Panzer and two infantry divisions. The XXII Corps and two mountain divisions were still arriving and would join the attack later.

Army Group South reserves would comprise one infantry division of the VII Corps, and five other infantry divisions. The reserve corps would follow Tenth Army in the attack, behind the XV Corps. Two of the other five infantry divisions would be disposed at the junction of Eighth and Tenth Armies, one would be disposed in the area of Tenth Army, and two at the junction of Tenth and Fourteenth armies.

In the west, Army Group C had been mobilized and become operational at the same time as the army groups on the Polish frontier, with Generaloberst Hitter von Leeb, recalled from retirement, in command. 12 active, six second-wave, 12 third-wave and three fourth-wave divisions comprised Leeb's defence force, supported by the Second Air Force in the north and the Third Air Force in the south. This would hardly suffice to hold a general attack by the French Army, supported by the British Army and Royal Air Force. However, even though the OKH planners did not share Hitler's optimism and were convinced France and Britain would declare war in the event of an attack on Poland, they felt that the Allies would be hesitant to attack and that the Wehrmacht would be able to achieve a quick victory in Poland. The Westwall defences, meanwhile, would discourage any British and French offensive until German troops could be shifted from Poland to the west.

On the eve of operations, Germany had all of its divisions under arms. The bulk of the Army, including all of Germany's panzer, motorized, and light divisions, was concentrated in the east. In the west, a minimum force, all infantry divisions, held the Westwall against a possible French and British attack. The remainder of the German ground force, a few reserve infantry divisions, was scattered about in the interior of the Reich.

The strength figures for the German ground forces in the east included 630,000 men in Army Group North and 886,000 in Army Group South. Of the Army Group North total, 320,000 were in the Third Army and 230,000 in Fourth Army; the remaining 80,000 comprised army group troops or units retained under the direct control of OKH. Of the Army Group South total, 180,000 were with Eighth Army, 300,000 with Tenth Army, and 210,000 with Fourteenth Army; the remaining 196,000 were army group or OKH troops.

No unforeseen incidents arose to disrupt preparations. The weather remained clear as the troops closed in their final assembly areas for the attack.

CHAPTER 7

The Attack Opens

The German attack was a tactical surprise to the Polish Army, despite both the troop concentrations the Polish High Command knew were taking place beyond the frontier and the worsening diplomatic situation. The Polish Government had ordered a general mobilization on 30 August, but many reservists were still en route to join their organizations and some units were in the process of movement to concentration areas or defensive positions when the Wehrmacht commenced operations. Hitler's headquarters, OKW, was in Berlin at the time of the attack, while OKH directed the Army effort from a field headquarters at Zossen, outside the Reich capital.

The German Air Force commenced hostilities at 0440 by bombing Polish air bases at widely separated points throughout the country. A few minutes later the Schleswig-Holstein commenced shelling the Polish fortress of Westerplatte in Danzig Harbor at a range of only several hundred yards. The brief but heavy bombardment was followed by the landing of a small German force, which was immediately driven off by the Poles.

The Polish destroyer Wicker was sunk defending the port of Gdynia against air attack and bombardment by light German naval units. All five Polish submarines were at sea; three

Warsaw: an aerial photograph of one of the forts which ringed the city.

escaped to internment in Sweden, while the Orzel and Wilk managed to reach safety in Britain. In the waters offshore, German surface, submarine, and air forces quickly established a tight blockade of the Polish port areas.

German ground troops at some points exchanged fire with Polish Army patrols and border police as the Army crossed the frontier. This scattered resistance was quickly overcome and the Poles were forced to withdraw before superior German force and firepower. The German ground forces experienced the usual confusion of troops coming under fire for the first time. Incidents were reported of artillery and tanks firing on friendly forces. Despite a number of minor reverses, fire discipline and control by unit commanders were quickly established and German ground operations proceeded on schedule.

At 10:00 on 1st September Hitler reported the opening of hostilities to the assembled Reichstag in the Kroll Opera House in Berlin. According to Hitler, the Wehrmacht was defending German territory and taking necessary counteraction to an organized Polish attack. The Führer stated further that he had no quarrel with Great Britain or France, and was desirous of reaching agreement with both western powers. Hitler also announced that in the event he were to become a casualty, his successor would be Hermann Goering, a clear indication of the degree of authority Hitler had attained over Germany.

The opening battles

Visibility was limited by a heavy mist the morning of 1st September as Bock's Army Group North moved into Poland. Third Army debouched from East Prussia in a drive south on Warsaw with its I Corps and Corps Wodrig in line, and southwestward on Grudziadz with its XXI Corps. Fourth Army attacked eastward across The Corridor from Pomerania, and Danzig was taken without a struggle by Brigade Eberhard.

Simultaneously one of the iconic actions of World War II was unfolding. The Polish Post Office (Poczta Polska) in the Free City of Danzig was created in 1919 under the Treaty of Versailles, and its buildings were considered extraterritorial Polish property. It had become a symbol of Polish ambitions in an overwhelmingly German city.

On September 1st 1939, Polish militiamen defended the Polish post office building for some fifteen hours against a series of assaults by the vastly superior forces of the SS Heimwehr Danzig supported by local SA formations and special units of Ordnungspolizei (Danzig police). All but four of the defenders who escaped from the building during the surrender were later sentenced to death by a German military court as partisans on October 5th, 1939 and executed.

The Polish Post Office in Danzig actually comprised several buildings. In 1930 the "Gdańsk 1" building on Heweliusz Square in the Old Town became the primary Polish post office, with a direct telephone line to Poland. In 1939 it employed slightly over 100 people. A number of the employees serving at the Polish Post Office also belonged to a Polish self-defence and security organization, and many were also members of the Polish Zwiàzek Strzelecki (Riflemen's Association). According to the testimony of the survivor Edmund Charaszkiewicz, the SS were right to target the post office as the Polish Post Office was from 1935 an important component of the Polish Intelligence organization, "Group Zygmunt."

As tensions between Poland and Germany increased the Polish High Command detached engineer and Army Reserve Sublieutenant Konrad Guderski to the Baltic Sea coast. He arrived in April 1939 and along with Alfons Flisykowski and others, he helped organize the official and volunteer security staff at the Polish Post Office and prepare them for eventual hostilities. In addition to training the staff, he prepared the defences in and around the building: nearby trees were removed, and the entrance was fortified. In mid-August, ten additional employees were sent to the post office from Polish Post offices in Gdynia and Bydgoszcz (mostly reserve non-commissioned officers).

In the building of the Polish post on 1st September there were 57 people: Konrad Guderski, 42 local Polish employees, ten employees from Gdynia and Bydgoszcz, and the building keeper with his wife and ten-year old daughter who lived in the building. Polish employees had a cache of weapons, including three Browning wz.1928 light machine guns, 40 other firearms and three chests of hand grenades. The Polish defence plan assigned the defenders the role of keeping Germans from the building for 6 hours, when a relief force from Armia Pomorze was supposed to secure the area.

The German attack plan, devised in July 1939, devised that the building defenders would be stormed from two directions. A diversionary attack was to be carried out at the front entrance, while the main force would break through the wall from the neighbouring Work Office and attack from the side. At 04:00 Germans cut the phone and electricity lines to the building. At 04:45, just as the German battleship Schleswig-Holstein started shelling the nearby Polish Army military outpost at Westerplatte, German forces began their assault on the Polish Post. German units detached for this task were composed of the special unit of

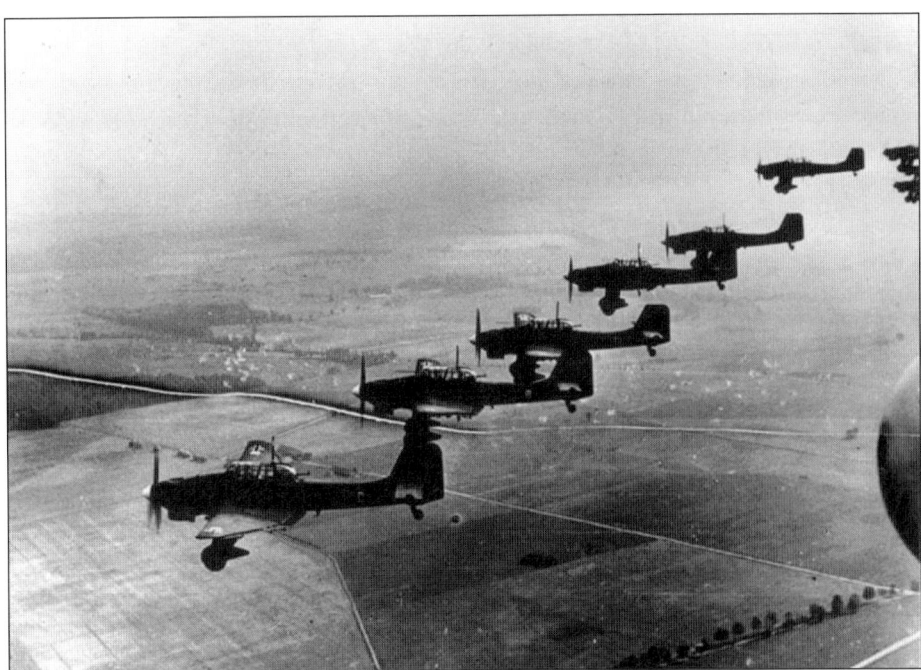

Stukas flying in formation over Poland

The light riveted armour of the Polish light tanks was easily pierced even by the low velocity weapons available to the Wehrmacht.

Danzig police, local SA formations and the SS units SS Wachsturmbann "E" and SS Heimwehr Danzig, supported by at least three ADGZ heavy armoured cars. The attack was commanded by German police colonel, Willi Bethke.

The first German attack, from the front, was repelled, although Germans managed to break through the entrance and briefly enter the building (at the cost of two killed and seven wounded attackers, including one group leader). The second attack, from the Work Office, was also repelled. The commander of Polish defence, Konrad Guderski, died during that second attack from the blast of his own grenade which stopped the Germans who broke through the wall.

At 11:00 German units were reinforced by the Wehrmacht with two 75 mm artillery pieces, but the second attack, even with the artillery support, was again repulsed. At 15:00 Germans declared a two-hour ceasefire and demanded that Polish forces surrender, which they refused. In the meantime, Germans received additional reinforcements: a 105 mm artillery piece, and a unit of sappers, which dug under the walls and prepared a 600 kg explosive device. At 17:00 the bomb was set off, collapsing part of the wall, and German forces under the cover of three artillery pieces attacked again, this time capturing most of the building with the exception of the basement.

At 18:00 Germans brought automatic pumps, gasoline tanks and flamethrowers, which they used to flood the basements with burning gasoline. After three Poles were burned alive (bringing the total Polish casualties to six killed in action), the rest decided to capitulate. The first two people to leave the building — director Dr. Jan Michof, carrying a white flag, and commandant (naczelnik) Józef Wàsik — were shot by the Germans (according to one version, Dr. Michof was attacked with a flamethrower). The rest of the Poles were allowed to surrender and leave the burning building. Six people managed to escape from the building, although two of them were captured the following days.

At army level things were proceeding equally well. Rapid progress was made during the morning of 1 September on the Third Army front. During the afternoon the Third Army force moving on Warsaw encountered strong resistance from the Polish 8th and 20th Infantry Divisions and the Novogrodsha Cavalry Brigade in the Mlawa area. Polish light tanks and tankettes were the first opponents for the German Panzers outclassed and outnumbered Polish tank crews fought bravely and managed to destroy a number of German vehicles before they bowed to the inevitable. The German tank attacks were finally stopped with heavy loss by antitank fire from Mlawa's concrete fortifications.

Fourth Army engaged elements of the Pomorska Cavalry Brigade at the outset of operations in The Corridor, but the Polish cavalrymen withdrew before the German advance. By noon it was apparent to Fourth Army that the Pomorze Army was attempting to withdraw to the south and east. Later in the afternoon elements of the Polish 9th Infantry Division were also identified on the Fourth Army front. Army group intelligence estimated that the Poles were much weaker in The Corridor than anticipated, though they were still believed capable of making a stand behind the Brda (Brahe) River, dividing the lower Corridor.

Third Army operations, 2nd September

Tczew (Dirschau) was taken by an engineer task force of Third Army at dawn on 12 September, but the city's vital bridge across the Vistula was destroyed by the Poles. The task force, known as Group Medem, was unable to seize a crossing and Army Group North had to direct other units to effect crossings at Gniew (Mewe) and near Marienwerder. Third Army's XXI Corps fought off heavy Polish counterattacks in its advance toward Grudziadz on 2 September. The bridge across the Vistula at Grudziadz was kept under artillery fire to prevent crossing the Poles and the corps prepared to make concerted attacks against the city from north and east the following day.

On the Mlawa front I Corps failed to make any further progress, but Corps Wodrig units broke through Polish field fortifications east of the fortress city and pushed south. Panzer Division Kempf was promptly detached from the I Corps and shifted eastward to support Corps Wodrig in its advance. The Third Army plan for the force moving on Warsaw was quickly revised. Corps Wodrig was to execute an enveloping movement to take the Polish units defending Mlawa in the rear, while the 1st Cavalry Brigade secured the exposed left of the corps as it turned in its swing to the west. The two corps and the cavalry brigade would resume their southward movement in line after destroying the Polish force at Mlawa or compelling it to withdraw.

Fourth Army operations, 2nd September

Fourth Army crossed the Brda during the second day of hostilities, advancing within a few miles of the Vistula. The apprehensions about a strong Polish defence line along the Brda did not materialize. The success of the German advance was threatened for a few hours, however, when Panzer elements of XIX Corps outran their gasoline and ammunition supply. The Poles failed to gain any but a temporary advantage from this situation, and German supply columns fought their way through withdrawing Polish units to the stalled tanks.

Fourth Army gains of 2nd September sealed off the Pomorze Army's 9th Infantry Division and Pomorska Cavalry Brigade, and the 27th Infantry Division, which had been identified farther east in The Corridor. The two Polish infantry divisions were destroyed in a number of attempts to escape through the line formed by the German forces that had crossed the base of The Corridor. The cavalry brigade was shattered by XIX Corps' armour, but there were no charges pitting mounted lancers against tanks. The Polish Campaign is surrounded by numerous myths such as Polish Cavalry charges against German armoured units which appear to have been an invention of the German and even Italian propaganda and are very far from truth. Polish cavalry was active during the campaign and acted as horse mounted infantry. One of the most successful cavalry charges took place at Krojanty, where elements of 18th Uhlans Regiment attacked and destroyed German infantry battalion only to be counterattacked by German armoured unit. Uhlans attempted to withdraw and suffered heavy losses. This event lead to the story of Polish cavalry charges on panzers. Polish cavalry brigades never charged tanks with their sabres or lances as they were equipped with anti-tank weapons such as 37mm Bofors wz.36 (model 1936) anti-tank guns (that could penetrate 26mm armour at 600m at 30 degrees). The cavalry brigades were in the process of being reorganized into motorized brigades.

The Polish Air Force was actually deployed at numerous airfields at the outset of the campaign and although numerically inferior and partially obsolete was very active during the course of the campaign which continued until September 14th over Warsaw. It is widely accepted that Polish pilots shot down around 140 Luftwaffe planes. Despite some Polish successes in minor border battles, German technical, operational and numerical superiority soon forced the Polish armies to retreat from the borders towards Warsaw and Lwów. The Luftwaffe quickly gained air superiority early in the campaign. By destroying communications, the Luftwaffe increased the pace of the advance which soon overran Polish airstrips and early warning sites and causing logistical problems for the Poles. Many Polish Air Force units ran low on supplies, 98 of their number withdrew into then-neutral Romania. The Polish initial strength of 400 aircraft was reduced to just 54 by September 14th and air opposition virtually ceased.

The junction of Third and Fourth Armies

The 10th Panzer Division of the army group reserve was shifted to the northeast across Fourth Army's rear on 2nd September. Bock planned to effect a crossing in the northern area of The Corridor with a strong Panzer force as soon as possible.

Third Army's XXI Corps identified the Pomorze Army's 16th Infantry Division in the Grudziadz area on 3rd September, and its 4th Infantry Division to the east of the city. Heavy air attacks on the 4th Infantry Division broke up the Polish threat to the left flank of XXI Corps, and the corps continued to advance southwestward to drive out the Polish 16th Infantry Division and enter Grudziadz. Despite heavy losses, the two Polish divisions succeeded in withdrawing in good order to the south and east, while rear guards fought a strong delaying action within the city itself.

A tank crew in a Panzer III. A Panzer IV with the low velocity infantry support gun can be seen in the background.

On the Mlawa front the Mazowiecka Cavalry Brigade was identified before Third Army's Corps Wodrig. The I Corps, supported by the attack of Corps Wodrig from the east, broke into the Mlawa defences and forced the stubborn defenders to withdraw.

Fourth Army sent the 10th Panzer Division across The Corridor just below Danzig and into East Prussia immediately upon the division's attachment from army group reserve on 3rd September. The 207th Infantry Division turned to the north after the Panzer units had passed, and forced the Polish forces still in the upper area of The Corridor to withdraw toward Gdynia. Other Fourth Army units cleared the area of the lower Corridor, established contact with Third Army units at Nowe Swiecie (Neuenburg), and launched a series of heavy attacks against the Pomorze Army's 15th Infantry Division in position north of Bydgoszcz.

The first phase of the campaign in the north was completed on 3rd September with the linking of the Third and Fourth Armies. The Pomorze Army force assigned to the defence of The Corridor proper had been destroyed, with a loss of 15,000 men in prisoners alone, 90 field pieces, and large stocks of matériel. The Modlin Army, from which the Germans claimed to have captured 10,000 prisoners, had been forced to withdraw southward from the Mlawa area. The Corridor was cut at base and center. The northern end of The Corridor and the fortress of Westerplatte in Danzig Harbor remained in Polish hands, but under constant attack by German ground, air, and sea forces. The Podlaska Cavalry Brigade of the Narew Group made several local penetrations into East Prussia in the area held by Corps Brand during this period of operations. These actions received much publicity in the foreign press but affected the campaign very little.

The political decision to defend the border was not the Polish high command's only strategic mistake. Polish pre-war propaganda stated that any German invasion would be

Soviet forces easily achieved their objectives and the conquest and partition of Poland was complete within a month.

easily repelled, so that the eventual Polish defeats in the September Campaign came as a shock to many civilians, who were unprepared for such news and, with no training for such a disaster, panicked and retreated east, spreading chaos, lowering troop morale and making road transportation for Polish troops very difficult. The propaganda also had some negative consequences for the Polish troops, whose communications, disrupted by German mobile units operating in the rear and civilians blocking roads, were further thrown into chaos by bizarre reports from Polish radio stations and newspapers which often reported imaginary victories and other military operations. This led to some Polish troops being encircled or making a stand against overwhelming odds, when they thought they were actually counterattacking or would soon receive reinforcements from other victorious areas.

Army Group South, 1st-6th September: The advance to the Warta (Warthe)

The morning of 1st September was clear on the front of Rundstedt's Army Group South, which had the advantage of air reconnaissance as it moved into Poland. Eighth Army, on the left, advanced toward Lodz and protected Tenth Army's north flank. Tenth Army, in the center of the army group line, struck out in the direction of Warsaw with the strongest concentration of armour in either army group. Fourteenth Army, on the right, moved toward the industrial area about Cracow and into Galicia, protecting the south flank of the main attack force.

Forward elements of Army Group South penetrated three to four miles into Poland by 06:00. Steady progress was reported until 14:00, when the army group commander was informed that the retreating Poles had demolished numerous bridges and even blown up stretches of roadway to slow the German armoured and motorized columns. Tenth Army also reported resistance by rear guards, an engagement with elements of the Wolynska Cavalry Brigade, and several incidents of civilians firing on German troops.

No protracted resistance was encountered, and by late afternoon some Army Group South units had advanced as much as 15 miles. The tactics of the new war of movement were first demonstrated during this period of operations. When their armoured columns were fired upon or held up by obstacles, the Germans deployed their tank units off the roads and continued their forward move. When necessary, the Luftwaffe was called upon to support the advance by dive-bombing centers of Polish resistance. Polish units bypassed by the German armour were engaged by infantry units following the tanks.

Eighth Army reported the 10th Infantry Division of the Lodz Army withdrawing toward Kalisz (Kalisch) and the 14th and 25th Infantry Divisions and Wielkopolska Cavalry Brigade of the Poznan Army retreating to the north and east. Tenth Army reported the Polish 7th Infantry Division and Krakowska Cavalry Brigade of the Cracow Army and the 28th and 30th Infantry Divisions and Wolynska Cavalry Brigade of the Lodz Army to be withdrawing to the east. Most of the first day's fighting on the Eighth and Tenth Army fronts was carried on between Polish rear guards and German reconnaissance elements or the advance guard of German armoured and motorized units.

Fourteenth Army reconnaissance troops and Slovak units on the right of the army front captured a number of villages in the area immediately to the north of the Slovak frontier by the close of the first day. Other Fourteenth Army units drove elements of the Rzeszow Armoured Cavalry Brigade from the Novy Targ (Neumarkt) region, and cleared the Jablunka Pass and the area for several miles to the north of the pass of the Cracow Army's 21st Mountain Division after hard fighting. The Polish 5th Infantry Division from the general reserve and the 6th Infantry Division of the Cracow Army were forced to withdraw in the direction of Cracow, and the Cracow Army's 23rd Infantry Division fell back to the northeast of the city. Units on the left flank of Fourteenth Army then found themselves confronted by strong permanent fortifications guarding the approaches to the industrial complex in the southwest of Poland.

The attack of Army Group South was resumed at 06:00 on 2nd September. The Poles resisted stubbornly at Mikolow (Nibolai), in the fortifications before Katowice (Kattowitz), and about Czestochowa (Tschenstochau). Eighth Army crossed the upper Prosna, Tenth Army reached the Warta above Czestochowa in its zone of advance, and Fourteenth Army divisions fought their way forward to converge north of Novy Targ.

Their movements made it apparent to Rundstedt that the Poles intended to establish a defensive line along the Warta River, and hold out in such fortified areas as Katowice and Czestochowa as long as possible. The Germans also found an increasing number of demolitions and other obstacles to the movement of armoured and motorized units. A number of reservists sufficient to form two provisional divisions were sent to reinforce the Polish units facing Eighth Army. Elements of several infantry divisions from the Polish general reserve also moved into the area beyond the Warta in the Tenth Army's zone of advance.

Czestochowa was taken on the morning of 3rd September, and Tenth Army seized several bridgeheads across the Warta despite determined Polish resistance. Fourteenth Army fought its way through the fortifications about Katowice and Mikolow in its zone of advance, and moved east along the Vistula. The southern Polish armies, bypassed in numerous places by the fast-moving German columns, began a hurried withdrawal. The troops on the front noted a marked decrease in Polish resistance and made extensive gains.

The Advance across the Polish Plain and into Galicia

By the morning of 4th September Army Group South estimated the withdrawing Poznan Army incapable of launching a heavy attack on the exposed left flank of the Eighth Army as it advanced northeastward. Tenth Army had virtually destroyed the Cracow Army's 7th Infantry Division and taken 1,000 prisoners, including the division commander. Heavy losses had also been inflicted on the Krakowska Cavalry Brigade. Tenth Army's Panzer divisions continued the drive eastward, moving beyond Radomsko, while two light divisions protected the right flank of the Panzer units and advanced to the Pilica River. Fourteenth Army reported the destruction of the Cracow Army's 6th Infantry Division and a general Polish withdrawal toward Cracow and the east.

The XXII Corps was operational under Fourteenth Army control on 4th September and advancing northward in the Novy Targ sector, with a Panzer, a mountain, and a light division attached. The XVIII Corps, which had controlled these three divisions the morning of the attack, had been withdrawn to assume control of two mountain divisions on the right front of the army and make a crossing into Poland farther to the east.

Additional gains were reported by all three armies on 5th September. Eighth Army was advancing rapidly to the northeast, while its X Corps presented a front to the north. Several battalions of the IV Frontier Command, a regiment of the 62nd Infantry Division, and elements of the 252nd Infantry Division crossed the Reich frontier to fill the gap formed as Eighth Army moved farther eastward. The frontier command and the infantry units were immediately organized into a task force known as Group Gienanth and given responsibility for the defence of Army Group South's exposed left flank. As Eighth Army continued to move eastward the front presented by the X Corps became more extended despite the relief afforded by the commitment of Group Gienanth. The Poznan Army to the north had not been engaged as heavily as the other Polish armies in the frontier area and still possessed a considerable combat potential.

Tenth Army units were across the Pilica by 5th September, and the way was open for an advance across the Polish Plain to the capital. The Polish reserves had been committed and there were a few units to be drawn upon to reinforce the sagging defence line before Warsaw.

Fourteenth Army drove eastward on Cracow against stiffening resistance on 5th September. The XXII Corps below the Vistula moved in the direction of the San River, and the XVIII Corps fought a way into Poland through the eastern Carpathian passes.

Rundstedt's headquarters revised its earlier estimate of the Poznan Army's capabilities on the Eighth Army flank on 6th September and prepared to meet a Polish attack from the north. The army group commander requested additional cavalry for reconnaissance purposes but

A column of motorized German troops advances deeper into Poland.

The view from the machine gunner's position of a Heinkel 111 over a Polish city.

OKH could make no cavalry available. To restrict the Poznam Army's movement and channel its withdrawal, two infantry divisions of the army group reserve were sent into line between X Corps and Group Gienanth, strengthening that part of the Eighth Army front facing north.

Tenth Army continued to move northeastward on a wide front on 6 September, making deep penetrations with its Panzer divisions. The Poles contested the advance of the Panzer divisions bitterly, since they were closest to Warsaw and threatened the eastward retreat of the Lodz and Poznan Armies. The Panzer divisions were followed by infantry divisions, which quickly cleared the captured areas of bypassed Polish units and stragglers. The Panzer division on the northern flank beat off heavy counterattacks, inflicted severe losses on the Poles, and captured the commander of the Polish general reserve's 29th Infantry Division. Fourteenth Army captured the key city of Cracow the same day.

Intelligence reports indicated that the Poles were attempting to rally remnants of their Cracoxo Army in the area of Radom. The destruction of the forces concentrating at Radom and known to still be at Lodz would prevent the escape of more organized Polish units beyond the Vistula River. Eighth Army was directed to make a frontal attack against the force assembling near Lodz. Tenth Army was ordered to envelope the force at Radom from north and south while continuing the drive toward the Vistula.

Meanwhile an order from OKH assigned Fourteenth Army the mission of destroying the Polish forces escaping to the east of the Vistula. Strong armoured and motorized forces were to move to the northeast in the direction of Lublin. Polish units that managed to escape destruction west of the Vistula would be caught within this second envelopment in eastern Poland.

The first phase of Army Group South's operations was completed by 6th September. The

Poznan Army had been forced to withdraw eastward. The Lodz Army was under heavy attack. Cracow had been taken and remnants of the Cracow Army at Radom were about to be enveloped by Tenth Army. The Carpathian Army had been forced to withdraw toward Lublin and Lwow.

No great number of prisoners had been taken in a single engagement, as had happened in The Corridor to the north a few days earlier. However, Army Group South reported several thousand captives in the Cracow area, and Tenth Army had bypassed thousands of Polish troops in its advance across the Warta; these were still being captured by the infantry units that had followed the armour. The Poles had also committed a larger proportion of their general reserve to stem the rapid advance of the stronger southern army group and to meet the threat Kundstedt posed to the capital and control center of the Polish defence effort. Tenth Army had had innumerable obstacles with which to contend, as the Poles destroyed bridges and other construction before its tank columns, and part of Fourteenth Army had had to fight its way through mountain passes defended by picked Polish mountain troops.

To retain control of its widening and moving front Army Group South displaced its headquarters to Lubliniec (Lublinitz), just inside the Polish frontier. Eighth Army moved to Gross Wartenberg, Tenth Army to Radomsko, and Fourteenth Army to Bielsko (Bielitz).

The Air Force and Navy

The mass air attacks in the opening hours of the war destroyed a large part of the Polish Air Force on the ground. Major bases at Warsaw, Grudziadz, Torun, Lodz, Czestochowa, Radom, Katowice, and Cracow were bombed heavily. Some German aircraft were brought down by the few Polish fighters that managed to get into the air, but the Polish planes were soon destroyed or driven off, and had to land at remote bases to refuel. Antiaircraft and small arms fire against low-flying German aircraft was reported as fairly accurate, while antiaircraft fire against bombers flying at medium and higher altitudes was reported as ineffective. The German aircraft proved themselves technically superior to the Polish types in the few reported instances of air-to-air combat.

In addition to these longer-range missions, the Luftwaffe bombed all known landing strips and a number of military installations in the border area, and rendered the Army some close support. Polish fortifications on the Tenth Army front were bombed the first day, expediting Tenth Army's advance toward the Warta.

Air attacks on the Polish naval vessels and antiaircraft emplacements in the harbor of Gdynia and on the antiaircraft defences of Hela completed the neutralization of these installations. Dive bombing attacks against the heavy fortifications of the Westerplatte in Danzig Harbor were unsuccessful and soon suspended.

German aircraft returned to base only long enough to refuel and secure more bombs and ammunition. Some German aircraft returned to the attack on the ground facilities of the Polish Air Force while other air units, their original mission accomplished, flew off to disrupt the movement of Polish reinforcements to the front and prevent the withdrawal of those units already committed against the Germans. Poland's east-wrest rail lines and the rail lines from the south to Gdynia were bombed heavily.

Air observation in support of the German ground forces operated under difficulties peculiar to the terrain and Polish population. German airmen had difficulty distinguishing German and Polish columns because of the heavy dust clouds thrown up from the unimproved roadways over which many units had to move. Thousands of Polish civilians also took to the roads before the German advance, wagons filled high with household goods and belongings. Moving alone in a cloud of dust, these refugee wagon trains resembled the horse-drawn columns of either Army.

A number of light attacks were made by the Polish Air Force. Several involved the participation of Polish aircraft in the air defence of Warsaw and in support of Polish ground units engaged with the German Tenth Army. One bombing attack was made on East Prussia. Several observation missions and fighter sorties were made over Silesia and Bohemia-Moravia, but the Polish Air Force had ceased to exist as an effective fighting force by 3rd September. The German First and Fourth Air Forces from that date were free to direct their major effort to the support of the ground forces.

In three days the Luftwaffe had driven the Polish Air Force from the skies, destroyed most of its bases on the ground, and crippled aircraft repair and production facilities. The mobilization of the Polish Army was disrupted by attacks on troop concentration areas and transportation lines. The damage of the first day to the Polish railroads was quickly repaired, but the release of more German aircraft from the task of destroying the Polish Air Force during the next few days made it possible to mount a series of attacks of increasing intensity against the Polish rail system; this interdiction was soon applied to the highways as well. German air units, after exhausting their bomb loads and ammunition, would keep moving columns on the roadways under observation until additional combat aircraft arrived to complete their destruction.

The German Navy played only a small part in operations with the light surface forces, the few submarines, and the old battleship Schleswig-Holstein that it committed to the Polish Campaign. When Great Britain and France declared war on 3rd September, the Führer countered with a directive ordering general mobilization of all the Reich's resources and permitting the Navy to engage in limited offensive operations. The Germans had already prepared for this eventuality by sending the bulk of their fleet to Atlantic and North Sea battle stations. Thus almost the entire German naval effort was concentrated against Great Britain from 3rd September, with little left for the few light Polish fleet units at large in the Baltic.

The Schleswig-Holstein remained in the Danzig Bay area, while submarines and destroyers blockaded Gdynia and Hela. Some support was rendered German ground forces in coastal areas, but for the most part the Navy in the Baltic had little to do except protect convoys moving from Stettin and other north German ports to East Prussia and prevent the escape of the few remaining Polish naval and merchant vessels.

CHAPTER 8

The Destruction of the Polish Army

T he fortunes of the Polish armies were symbolized by the garrison of the Westerplatte. On September 1st, 1939, at 0445 local time, as Germany began its invasion of Poland, Schleswig-Holstein started to shell the Polish garrison of the Westerplatte in Danzig. This was followed by an attack by German naval infantry which was repelled. Another two assaults that first day were also repelled. Over the course of the next seven days, the German forces repeatedly bombarded Westerplatte with naval and heavy field artillery along with dive-bombing raids by Junkers Ju 87 Stukas. Repeated attacks of 3,500 German soldiers were repelled by the 180 Polish soldiers for the next seven days. Finally commander Major Henryk Sucharski was informed that no help from the Polish Army would come. On September 7th Major Henryk Sucharski decided to surrender due to lack of ammunition and supplies. As a sign of honor for the soldiers of Westerplatte, German commander, Gen. Eberhardt, allowed Mjr. Sucharski to keep his officer's sword while being taken prisoner.

At the strategic level the speed of the German advance made effective direction and coordination of the Polish defence effort increasingly difficult as operations continued. The declaration of war by Great Britain and France on 3rd September did not bring with it the relief the Polish High Command had expected. The Hitler directive immediately following the declaration had left the opening of offensive operations in the air and on the ground to the British and French, and it was only a question of time until the German Army would

Himmler in discussion with Muller, Heydrich, Nebe and Huber

A field howitzer deployed in the front line.

overrun Poland.

An attempt was made to reorganize the battered Polish forces into three armies, one north of the Vistula, a second holding the front from Warsaw to the junction of the Vistula and San Rivers, and the third in the south. The rapid advance of the Germans prevented implementation of this plan.

The two German army groups exerted pressure on the Poznan Army from north and south and forced it to continue its withdrawal eastward. Remnants of the Pomorze Army also fell back before the Third and Fourth Armies on the withdrawal route followed by the Poznan Army. Some units of the Lodz Army, under heavy attack by the Eighth Army, were also forced to withdraw in the general direction of Warsaw. The road and rail network of the Polish Plain west of Warsaw was to cause a convergence of these various forces in the area about Kutno. Tenth Army pushed remnants of the Cracow Army back into the Radom area, while other units of the Cracow Army and the Carpathian Army were forced to retreat toward the Lublin area and Lwow before Fourteenth Army. In the extreme north some units of the Narew Group withdrew in the direction of Brzesc to avoid being outflanked.

The second phase of German operations consisted of destroying these remaining major Polish forces. German armoured units disregarded their exposed flanks and raced ahead of the infantry divisions to cut the retreating Polish armies into smaller groups. The Luftwaffe complete control of the air and was able to keep withdrawing Polish columns under constant observation and attack. Forests areas occupied by Polish units were set afire with incendiaries and the troops attacked from the air when they fled into the open. The national government at Warsaw prepared for movement to the south and east, where it might continue the war or escape to Romania.

The German successes against the Polish Army were dampened by the situation in the west. Britain and France might go over to the offensive at any time, and they held the advantage as long as the bulk of the German Army and the Luftwaffe were committed in Poland. As OKH viewed the situation, it was imperative that operations in Poland be brought to a conclusion as speedily as possible, and that the bulk of the German forces be shifted to the west. The Luftwaffe would have little difficulty in moving its air units from the east to the large number of bases in the west. The army, however, with its far larger force and with its tanks and artillery, required more transportation and time to shift from one theater of war to another. As a consequence, OKH was opposed to any proposal to move deeper into Poland than was necessary to effect the destruction of the Polish Army. This strategic plan of OKH was opposed by Bock and Guderian, who were eager to make a deep armoured penetration into eastern Poland to prevent the escape of major Polish forces into the Pripyat Marshes area.

A number of the usual reports on atrocities by both sides made their appearance during this period. One that received a great amount of publicity occurred on Sunday, 3rd September, when Polish troops at Bydgoszc claimed to have been fired upon by minority Germans. A number of German civilians resident in the Bydgoszcz area were shot in an operation directed by the local Polish commander, and the Reich government charged the Polish Government with terrorism. The Polish Government, in turn, used the incident to support its claim of fifth column activities on the part of the German minority resident within Poland's borders. The "Bloody Sunday" incident was promptly used in the psychological warfare effort of both Germans and Poles.

Army Group North, 4th-17th September
Operations in western Poland

Third Army reported its XXI Corps in firm control of Grudziadz on 4th September. Engineers immediately set to work repairing the bridges across the Vistula, to establish a further linkup with Fourth Army.

On the left of the Third Army front I Corps and Corps Wodrig regrouped to resume their southward advance from Mlawa. The army group was critical of the operations just concluded at Mlawa, taking the position that Third Army should have bypassed the Polish defences. Little resistance was encountered immediately south of Mlawa, but a stiff defence was expected along the Narew River.

Fourth Army opened the second phase of operations with its XIX Corps clearing the area west of the Vistula near Grudziadz of Polish units still trying to escape from The Corridor. Reaching the river, the XIX Corps moved northward. Other Fourth Army units south of Grudziadz crossed the Vistula the same day, while fighting a series of actions with the remnants of Polish units that had infiltrated through the XIX Corps. At the base of The Corridor Fourth Army forced the Pomorze Army's 15th Infantry Division to withdraw from its positions north of Bydgoszcz.

With The Corridor operation completed Army Group North began to plan the movement of the bulk of Fourth Army to the east flank of the army group front. This movement would enable Army Group North to clear its left front of Polish forces and execute a wide encirclement east of Warsaw. Bock understood that he had the authority to order such a major move as a result of a telephone conversation with Brauchitsch on 2nd September. According to the army group plan, Fourth Army would move on Lomza, from concentration areas in East Prussia east of Third Army, and drive south to destroy the Polish forces on the left flank of the army group front. This accomplished, Fourth Army would move west to envelop other Polish forces still facing Third Army. Some risk would be involved in stripping The Corridor area and the region immediately to the south of combat units. Polish remnants would be left far behind the German battle line, opposed only by security troops and service units.

Army Group North was obliged to revise its plan with the receipt of orders from OKH on 4th September and during the night of 4-5th September. In the first of the two orders, OKH authorized the organization of only a small provisional force of fortress troops and reservists from units already available in East Prussia to move on Lomza. The second order directed the Fourth Army to continue its drive on Warsaw from the northwest. Panzer and motorized units (XIX Corps) could be shifted to the left front of Third Army, but would have to remain west of the line Ostrow Mazowiecka-Warsaw in the drive on the Polish capital.

Army Group North still held that its left should be strengthened further. A call by Bock to Brauchitsch the morning of 5th September confirmed the OKH order. The commander in chief of the Army gave as reason for his decision the belief that the Poles no longer had an effective army. Despite Bock's remonstrations, OKH would permit no moves further eastward than were necessary, in view of Germany's weak situation along the Westwall.

An additional link was established between the Third and Fourth Armies southeast of Grudziadz on 6th September, and the German line across the Southeastern area of The Corridor was shortened. The XIX Corps headquarters and one division were immediately withdrawn and moved to the left flank of Third Army, where the corps would organize the provisional force OKH had authorized for the move on Lomza. Army Group North moved its headquarters to Allenstein in East Prussia the same day, and remained there to the end of the campaign. Third Army moved to the frontier area south of Allenstein and Fourth Army shifted to a point within The Corridor northwest of Bydgoszcz.

Operations in eastern Poland

The XXI Corps concentrated in the Pisia (Pisseck) River area on its return to East Prussia, and was redesignated Group Falkenhorst, after its commander. The 10th Panzer Division was added to Falkenhorst's command, which was to consist of an armoured division, an infantry division, and a brigade of fortress troops and reservists from East Prussia. Army Group North was apprehensive, and felt that Group Falkenhorst would not be strong enough to accomplish its mission. Moreover, the commitment of Group Falkenhorst would draw the attention of the Poles to the area in which the army group planned to concentrate the Panzer and motorized divisions of XIX Corps for a fast drive deep into eastern Poland. Despite army group's misgivings, Group Falkenhorst was committed on 7th September, when it moved south on Lomza with the 10th Panzer Division, followed by the brigade of East Prussian troops.

The effect of a direct bomb hit on a Polish train.

Army Group North received a welcome but premature message from Rundstedt's headquarters the evening of 8 September. According to Army Group South, the XVI Corps had taken Warsaw and established several crossings on the Vistula. The entry in the headquarters journal of Army Group North noted that "The drama is approaching its finale." The hope of a quick victory was dashed when it was learned that only one division had reached Warsaw and had been forced to withdraw, and that no crossing had been made along the Vistula.

The face of battle

The 20th Motorized Infantry Division arrived as the first of the XIX Corps units in East Prussia and concentrated in the rear of Group Falkenhorst. Corps headquarters itself arrived the day Group Falkenhorst was committed. The XIX Corps was retained under army group control and prepared to enter the battle against the Narew Group without waiting for the rest of its divisions. The 10th Panzer Division and East Prussian brigade were relieved from attachment to Group Falkenhorst and attached to the XIX Corps. Guderian quickly formed a line on the left of Group Falkenhorst and moved south on 9 September, followed by the 20th Motorized Infantry Division. Group Falkenhorst, having lost its armoured striking force to the XIX Corps, resumed the use of its original designation as the XXI Corps. The XIX Corps was able to report immediate progress southward, but the corps' left flank was completely uncovered and exposed to attack by the Podlaska Cavalry Brigade and other Narew Group units still in the Grodno area and about Bialystok.

The commitment of the XIX Corps on the Third Army front immediately posed another problem. The original boundary of Ostrow Mazowiecka, set for Third Army and Group

Falkenhorst, would seriously restrict the freedom of action of the fast-moving armoured units and prevent full exploitation of their capabilities. Army Group North requested OKH to assign another objective, suitable for the execution of a wide envelopment. The line Minsk Mazowiecki-Siedlce was settled upon. The army group planners felt that the area west of Siedlce was still too narrow for a sweeping envelopment east of Warsaw. However, it would suffice to form a link up with Army Group South east of the Vistula. Headquarters OKH remained firm in its decision to keep its forces as far to the west as possible.

The XIX Corps' 10th Panzer Division crossed the Narew at Wizna the day it attacked. The following morning the 20th Motorized Infantry Division crossed the river at a point some miles to the west. The corps commander was immediately ordered to move south across the Bug to intercept Polish forces withdrawing eastward from the Vistula.

The XXI Corps, on the right of the XIX Corps, was held up by Polish fortifications at Novgorod at the outset of the drive into eastern Poland. Though it managed to force the Polish 18th Infantry Division to withdraw, the XXI Corps could not maintain the pace of the advance set by the XIX Corps and fell behind.

The 20th Motorized Infantry Division became heavily engaged with elements of the Polish 18th Infantry Division in the vicinity of Zambrow on 10 September. Units of the 10th Panzer Division were diverted to assist the motorized division, and inflicted heavy losses on the Poles. The remainder of the 10th Panzer Division, followed by the 3rd Panzer Division, which had meanwhile rejoined the corps, penetrated to the Nurzyck (Nurzec) River, a tributary of the Bug, west of Bielsk.

Command control over the movements of these Panzer divisions and the motorized division was necessarily restricted to radio. The corps staff also experienced some difficulty in performing its proper function by reason of the frequent moves over long distances to keep the headquarters immediately behind the advancing divisions.

The southward movement of the XIX Corps also exposed its left flank to a Polish attack from the Bialystok area to the east. On 11 September Army Group North directed that Corps Brand secure this flank by a move against Bialystok. On the same day the 2nd Motorized Infantry Division began moving southward to rejoin XIX Corps, while the corps' 23rd Infantry Division remained in the border area.

Meanwhile I Corps and Corps Wodrig of Third Army moved rapidly toward the Bug after crossing the Narew. Advance elements of Corps Wodrig were across the Bug River by 10th September and drove south to intercept Polish units reported by air reconnaissance to be withdrawing eastward from Warsaw. Third Army headquarters moved to a new location southeast of Mlawa the same day.

Intelligence reports indicated that the Polish Government had fled to the Lwow area and that the Polish High Command had established headquarters in the fortress city. A large number of Polish units had managed to escape to the east of the Vistula, and it could therefore be expected that the Poles would attempt to establish a new defence line in southeastern Poland. A natural line already existed, from Brzesc down the Bug River to Lwow, thence to the west, and south along the San River to the Polish frontier. A deep drive into southeastern Poland would be necessary if this new defence line was to be destroyed before it could be completely organized.

Army Group South had already been ordered to move deeper into eastern Poland, in the direction of Lublin. Headquarters OKH on 11th September changed the objective of Army Group North to the line Kowela-Slonim. This would effect a second encirclement of Polish forces in the eastern part of the country, beyond the Bug River.

On 12th September OKH directed another change in the mission of Army Group North. The remnants of the Polish armies in the west were all but encircled about Kutno and in the area between that city and Warsaw. The army group's Third Army would be able to exert additional pressure on these Polish armies by investing Warsaw from the east and blocking escape from the city. Accordingly, OKH ordered Army Group North to execute a right turn with a part of its force and present a new front to the west. Third Army's I Corps was ordered to seize the river crossings into the city but to avoid becoming involved in a major engagement in the city itself, where house-to-house fighting would be costly in casualties and would prevent the disengagement of the corps when the expected order to resume the march to the southeast was received. Other Third Army forces would advance to the line Garwolin-Siedlce and establish a front to the southeast. The XIX Corps would drive east of the Bug and take Brzesc, to protect the left flank of the army group and make it possible to resume the army group advance into southeastern Poland with a minimum of delay.

The OKH order of 12th September also made Eighth Army responsible for operations at Kutno and released Fourth Army for movement to the east of the Army Group North front. Bock assigned Fourth Army responsibility for the security of the area in the direction of Bialystok, with Corps Brand and the XXI Corps attached.

The XIX Corps on 12th September controlled the 3rd and 10th Panzer Divisions and the 20th Motorized Infantry Division, and the 2nd Motorized Division had also rejoined the corps. The 10th Panzer Division led the advance on the left, followed by the 3rd Panzer Division, echeloned out to the left rear. On the right the 20th Motorized Division led the advance, followed at some distance by the 2nd Motorized Division, which was shifted to the rear of the 3rd Panzer Division the following day. The lack of infantry on the left of the armoured units was a cause of some concern at army group headquarters, since strong Polish forces were believed to be in the Pripyat Marshes and the heavily forested area to the east.

The difficulty in shifting units across the rear of XIX Corps in order to establish a front to the east was resolved by giving priority to XIX Corps. This involved some risk until the roads to the east were sufficiently clear of XIX Corps columns moving southward from East Prussia, but units of the Narew Group still west of Grodno and Bialystok were in no position to take advantage of the opportunity to attack the flank of the German columns en route to the south.

The Polish forces immediately east of Warsaw fought desperately but without coordination or direction of effort as Third Army's I Corps cleared the area to the Vistula. The army's Corps Wodrig reported the capture of 8,000 prisoners on 15th September alone as it moved southward. It was Bock's intention to direct the XIX Corps to send half of its force in the direction of Slonim to the northeast and the other half toward Kowela to the southeast after the capture of Brzesc. The commander of Army Group North estimated that

Ju52 support aircraft played a major role in keeping the Heer supplied.

infantry would require eight days to accomplish these missions, and the armoured and motorized units could reach the two objectives in a fraction of that time. Bock did not consider it necessary to commit any further forces to secure the vast Pripyat Marshes area.

The I Corps laid siege to the Warsaw suburb of Praga on 16th September. Farther south Corps Wodrig completed the destruction of Polish remnants that had fled across the Vistula from the Radom area before the Army Group South advance. The 1st Calvary Brigade patrolled the east bank of the Vistula to prevent further crossings by the Poles.

Fourth Army headquarters was operational southeast of Lomza on 16 September. This permitted Third Army to move its headquarters to Wegrow, where it could direct operations against Warsaw more closely. Bialystok was in German hands, and the Fourth Army front was secure as far south as Bielsk. Polish units identified on the front to the northeast indicated no threat to the army group's left flank.

Operations at Brzesc

On 14th September the 10th Panzer Division reported that its forward elements had reached Brzesc. The 3rd Panzer Division, which had shifted to the left rear of the 10th Panzer Division, covered the corps' left flank by pushing reconnaissance elements out in the direction of Kobryn. The corps commander hurried to join the force that had reached the objective, and the 20th Motorized Infantry Division, its operations against the Polish 18th Infantry Division completed, was shifted eastward to give the Panzer units at Brzesc additional infantry support.

Motorised German troops negotiate muddy conditions.

The initial German attack against Brzesc penetrated the city's outer fortifications, and the garrison withdrew into the fortress, known as the Citadel, that formed the core of the city's defensive system. An attempt to take the Citadel by a surprise attack was a failure, and Guderian decided that a determined assault by a larger force would be necessary.

On 16th September the 10th Panzer and 20th Motorized Infantry Divisions launched a concerted attack on the fortress, and took the outer line of defences. However, the infantry regiment of the 10th Panzer Division failed to advance immediately behind the artillery barrage laid down for its support, and the inner fortress remained in Polish hands.

The Citadel was finally taken on 17th September, when an infantry regiment of the 20th Motorized Infantry Division launched an assault as the Polish garrison was attempting to break out of the fortress and escape to the west. A total of 600 prisoners were taken by the Germans in this final phase of the Brzesc operation.

While the 10th Panzer and 20th Motorized Infantry Divisions were engaged in taking Brzesc, the 3rd Panzer Division moved around the city to the east and drove southward in the direction of Wlodowa.

The 2nd Motorized Infantry Division, following the 3rd Panzer Division, was assigned the mission of securing the left flank of the corps and moved eastward in the direction of Kobryn. The headquarters of the XIX Corps moved to Brzesc and prepared to meet the Russians, since the corps could not evacuate Brzesc before their arrival.

Active operations ended for part of the XIX Corps with the capture of Brzesc and its Citadel. The 10th Panzer and 20th Motorized Infantry Divisions remained in the Brzesc area. The 3rd Panzer Division, which had moved southward on Wlodowa, and the 2nd Motorized Division, moving on Kobryn to the east, were to continue their small actions, cutting off

Polish units attempting to escape eastward and taking numerous prisoners.

The 2nd Panzer Division of Army Group South was reported moving in the direction of Wlodowa. The XIX Corps was ordered to remain in place and be prepared to effect a junction with Rundstedt's army group. This order was never carried out and no link up of German forces was actually effected east of the Bug River. The 2nd Motorized Infantry Division shortly withdrew from Kobryn to rejoin the corps at Brzesc. The 3rd Panzer Division was also withdrawn on 20 September, as the corps made preparations to move to East Prussia. The XIX Corps was attached to Fourth Army the same day.

The intervention of the Russians

By 17th September 1939, the Polish defence was already broken, and the only hope was to retreat and reorganise along the Romanian bridgehead. However, these plans were rendered obsolete nearly overnight, when the over 800,000 strong Soviet Union Red Army entered and created the Belarussian and Ukrainian fronts after invading the eastern regions of Poland in violation of the Riga Peace Treaty, the Soviet-Polish Non-Aggression Pact, and other international treaties, both bilateral and multilateral. Soviet diplomacy claimed that they were "protecting the Ukrainian and Belarussian minorities of eastern Poland in view of Polish imminent collapse. Vyacheslav Molotov delivered a speech on 17th September 1939:

Events arising out of the Polish German War has revealed the internal insolvency and obvious impotence of the Polish state. Polish ruling circles have suffered bankruptcy... Warsaw as the capital of the Polish state no longer exists. No one knows the whereabouts of the Polish Government. The population of Poland have been abandoned by their ill-starred

The empty field of battle as viewed from a camouflaged German position.

A grenade is thrown in close quarter fighting.

leaders to their fate. The Polish state and its government have virtually ceased to exist. In view of this state of affairs, treaties concluded between the Soviet Union and Poland have ceased to operate. A situation has arisen in Poland which demands of the Soviet Government especial concern for the security of its state. Poland has become a fertile field for any accidental and unexpected contingency that may create a menace to the Soviet Union... Nor can it be demanded of the Soviet Government that it remain indifferent to the fate of its blood brothers, the Ukrainians and Byelorussians White Russians inhabiting Poland, who even formerly were without rights and who now have been abandoned entirely to their fate. The Soviet Government deems it its sacred duty to extend the hand of assistance to its brother Ukrainians and brother Byelorussians inhabiting Poland.

Polish border defence forces in the east, known as the Korpus Ochrony Pogranicza, consisted of about 25 battalions. Edward Rydz-Śmigły ordered them to fall back and not engage the Soviets. This, however, did not prevent some clashes and small battles, such as the Battle of Grodno, as soldiers and local population attempted to defend the city. The Soviets murdered numerous Poles, including prisoners of war like General Józef Olszyna-Wilczyński. The Organization of Ukrainian Nationalists rose against the Poles, and communist partisans organised local revolts, robbing and murdering Poles. Those movements were quickly disciplined by the NKVD. The Soviet invasion was one of the decisive factors that convinced the Polish government that the war in Poland was lost. Prior to the Soviet attack from the east, the Polish military's fall-back plan had called for long-term defence against Germany in the southern-eastern part of Poland, while awaiting relief from a Western Allies attack on Germany's western border. However, the Polish government refused to surrender or negotiate a peace with Germany. Instead, it ordered all units to evacuate Poland and reorganize in France.

Army Group North was informed of the Red Army's movement into eastern Poland by OKH early on 17th September, and was directed to remain west of the line along the Bug

River-Brzesc-Bialystok. Units of the XXI Corps in the Bialystok area and a motorized division of XIX Corps in the Brzesc region had already advanced east of this line. These units were to be permitted to remain east of the line long enough to complete their missions, after which they were to withdraw. The plan to send armoured and motorized infantry columns to Slonim and Kowela was abandoned. Despite the OKH order to confine its operations to the area west of the Bug-Brzesc-Bialystok line, Army Group North instructed its air reconnaissance units to continue flying missions to Grodno and other points deep enough to provide security for the army group.

The second phase of operations by Army Group North was completed with the intervention of the Red Army. All organized resistance in the area between Warsaw and Brzesc had ended, and Army Group North had established contact with Army Group South across the Vistula at Gora Kalwarja. Farther east advance Panzer units of XIX Corps had established radio contact with Panzer elements of Rundstedt's force and only a few miles separated the armoured spearheads of the two German army groups. Prisoners taken on 16th and 17th September represented half the identified Polish divisions and almost one-third of the cavalry brigades, and their statements indicated complete despair on the part of the remnants of the Polish Army. Hitler made a speech in the city of Danzig in which he said: "Poland never will rise again in the form of the Versailles treaty. That is guaranteed not only by Germany, but also... Russia."

Relations with the Russians suffered several setbacks at the outset in the Army Group North area. Russian aircraft bombed a bridge nine miles west of Bialystok on 17th September, killing three German soldiers and several Labor Service men. Other Russian air attacks inflicted casualties on advance units of XIX Corps east of the Bug.

Warsaw presented a special problem with the intervention of the Russians. The capital was held by a large garrison, reinforced by the units that had escaped encirclement in the battles farther west, and a large part of the heavy artillery required for an assault on Warsaw's defences was committed at Modlin, the fortress city a short distance down the Vistula. The bulk of the army group's armour was far to the east at Brzesc, and Hitler was unwilling to accept the heavy casualties an infantry assault on Warsaw would cost. However, the Führer was anxious to gain possession of the city before the arrival of the Russians, to impress the Red Army and prevent the formation of a Communist puppet government in the Polish capital.

To weaken the determination of the population of Warsaw to resist, a leaflet drop over the city had been made on 15th September, urging noncombatants to leave and promising fair treatment and the release of the garrison as soon as the formalities of surrender were completed. The Germans had to take into account the matter of foreign public opinion about the lives of noncombatants and the large diplomatic colony still inside Warsaw. The United States Congress was soon to convene in special session, and the Congress of American States had called on its members to meet. The killing of large numbers of civilians and disregard of accepted custom in repatriating diplomatic representatives would win the German Government no friends in either congress. The United States arms embargo was still in force, prohibiting the sale of weapons and munitions to the Allies, and the attitude of the American states toward the German attack was still undeclared.

Army Group South, 7th-17th September

All three of its armies reported progress as Army Group South entered the second phase of operations, and OKH cancelled its planned airborne attack on the Vistula crossing at Pulawy. The three army headquarters had to displace forward again to maintain proper control over their advancing units. On 7th September Eighth Army moved to the vicinity of Lodz, as it pressed the attack against that city and the Lodz Army. Tenth Army moved to Konskie on 9th September as it prepared to destroy forces of the Cracow Army concentrated Eadom. Fourteenth Army moved to a point southeast of Cracow the same day and continued its drive to the east and northeast. Army Group South moved its headquarters on 13th September to Kielce where it remained until the end of operations.

A series of separate battles developed on each of the army fronts. These were simultaneous actions, with each German army attempting to envelop and destroy the Polish units on its front and prevent their escape to the east.

Eighth Army

The combat potential of Eighth Army was increased considerably at the outset of the second phase of Army Group South's operations with the attachment of the XI and XVI Corps from Tenth Army. The XI Corps held the right of the army line, while XVI Corps reached the suburbs of Warsaw with its 4th Panzer Division on 8th September and its 1st Panzer Division penetrated to the Vistula.

The Eighth Army's successes against the Lodz Army and its deep penetration northeastward across the Polish Plain were to work to Eighth Army's temporary disadvantage in the area of the X Corps at the outset of the second phase of operations, however. The Gienanth Group and the 213th Infantry Division from the army group reserve on the army's north flank were left far to the west. The 221st Infantry Division from the army group reserve was disposed on a very wide front and was also too far to the west to come to the support of X Corps units in case of an attack from the north. The continued advance of Eighth Army to the northeast made necessary an increasing prolongation of the line held by X Corps against the Pozncm Army, particularly on the front of the German 30th Infantry Division.

The 30th Infantry Division made some redispositions to meet a possible attack, but was still in an unfavourable position for defence. Division units were strung out along an open flank for a distance of more than 20 miles and advancing northeastward in column, with only small detachments thrown out for security. The division artillery was scattered throughout the column and a coordinated defensive fire would have been impossible.

At noon on 10th September the German 30th Infantry Division reported itself under heavy attack from the north by a Polish force estimated at two or three infantry divisions and two cavalry brigades. The army commander first considered counterattacking with the XIII Corps, but discarded this plan in favour of directing the X Corps to turn its front to the north. The 30th Infantry Division lost some ground to the Poles, but the support of the other two infantry divisions of the corps made it possible to establish a new line the following day.

A number of antitank and other army group units were made available to Eighth Army

Stukas take off in yet another bombing run over Poland.

and hurried into line to bolster the front, and the XI Corps was directed to attack the Polish penetration on its eastern shoulder.

Despite the heavy losses incurred by the 30th Infantry Division, the Polish attack served the Germans in that it hastened the encirclement of the Poznan Army at Kutno. The diversion of units to make the attack weakened the eastern front of the Polish force and the XI Corps succeeded in driving the Poles to the west of the Bzura and farther away from Warsaw and Modlin and any possible escape to the two fortress cities.

On 11th September OKH placed Eighth Army in control of operations against the Polish forces about Kutno, and the army moved its headquarters to Lodz. The German plan for the operation provided for attacking the Poles from the west, south, and east, while Bock's army group blocked escape north across the Vistula. A day later OKH directed the attachment of the III Corps of Fourth Army south of the Vistula to the Eighth Army as Army Group North prepared to regroup and shift Fourth Army to the drive east of Warsaw. A provisional force was organized to hold the north bank of the Vistula against Polish crossings from the Kutno area.

Included in the Kutno encirclement at this time were 12 Polish divisions, including the Poznan Army's 14th, 17th, 25th, and 26th Infantry Divisions, and the Wielkopolska and Kresova Cavalry Brigades; remnants of the Lodz Army's 2nd, 10th, 13th, 28th and 30th Infantry Divisions and Wolynska Cavalry Brigade; and battered units of the Pomorze Army's 4th, 15th and 16th Infantry Divisions that managed to escape destruction following the junction of the German Third and Fourth Armies across the base of The Corridor. This represented more than one third of the entire Polish land force. Some concern was expressed at OKH and the headquarters of both army groups about the capability of this Polish force to break out to the east to join the garrison of Warsaw. For the next few days this encirclement, a development of the original OKH plan to destroy the bulk of the Polish armies west of the Vistula, was to become a focal point of attention in the campaign.

Eighth Army controlled a total of six corps for the operation against the Polish force at Kutno, including the XI and XVI Corps attached from Tenth Army. These corps were deployed in a rough circle about the Polish force centred between the Vistula and Bzura. One more attempt by the Poles to break out of the encirclement and escape to the southeast on 12th September was thwarted despite the loss of some ground by the Germans. The desperate attacks of the Poles only served to exhaust further their few units still intact.

The XI and XVI Corps reverted from Eighth to Tenth Army control on 15th September, as Tenth Army was made responsible for operations against Kutno from the east. The commander of the Polish force was finally identified as General Bortnowski, of the Poznan Army. Despite his hopeless position, Bortnowski made one more effort to break through the German line on 16 September, this time to the north and east in an attempt to cross the Vistula and reach Modlin. This final attempt was fruitless, and the Eighth Army took advantage of the weakening Polish situation to compress the Kutno force into a compact mass and a target small enough for a concentrated air assault.

The following day, 17th September, German air units attacking Warsaw were diverted long enough from their target to deliver a series of heavy air attacks on the encircled Poles and expedite the movement of ground units toward Kutno. The Polish defensive organization collapsed, and 40,000 prisoners were taken. A strong Polish force managed to fight its way through the German line and moved toward the forested area southwest of Modlin, below the Vistula. This force was immediately engaged by Tenth Army and destroyed.

At the conclusion of the second phase of Army Group South operations Eighth Army was still occupied in clearing the Kutno area of the last remnants of its Polish force. While Tenth Army completed the destruction of those Polish units that had escaped east of the Bzura, Eighth Army destroyed all those remaining west of the river. Since it was not in the area of the demarcation line between the Russian and German halves of the country and had no orders to move in that direction Eighth Army was not immediately affected by the sudden Russian advance into eastern Poland.

Tenth Army

The deep penetration of Tenth Army prevented the Polish forces near Radom from completing their defensive deployment as the second phase of Army Group South's operations began. The Lodz Army, already under attack by the Eighth Army on the German left, could not prevent Tenth Army tank units from moving up the north bank of the Pilica toward the Vistula and Warsaw. Bypassed on the south, the Lodz Army was forced to fall back on the Polish divisions at Kutno, and Tenth Army could make its major effort against the Polish force at Radom.

The Radom force on 8th September consisted of survivors of the Polish 3rd, 19th, and 29th Infantry Divisions from the general reserve, the Krakowska Cavalry Brigade and 7th Infantry Division of the Cracow Army, and the 12th Infantry Division from the general reserve. All but the 12th Infantry Division had been heavily engaged and had but a fraction of their original strength. Depleted as this force was, it succeeded in slowing the German advance toward the Vistula.

Tenth Army was directed by Rundstedt to destroy the Polish force at Radom by an envelopment from north and south. This would enable Tenth Army to seize crossings on the Vistula and press forward to a junction with Army Group North at Warsaw. The Tenth Army order of the same date assigned XIV and XV Corps the mission of enveloping the Polish force from the north and south, while IV Corps tied it down with attacks from the west and southwest.

Hard fighting developed as Panzer units reached the Vistula north and south of the Polish force at Radom late on 8th September. The stubborn resistance of the Poles required the full attention of Tenth Army, and the XI and XVI Corps on the left flank of Tenth Army were temporarily attached to Eighth Army.

Tenth Army destroyed the Polish force at Radom by 11th September and took 60,000 prisoners. A few Polish units of regimental strength withdrew into the more wooded areas and continued a sporadic resistance that tied down a number of German divisions for several more days. Bridges across the Vistula, including the important crossing at Pulawy, were secured. Tenth Army was directed to move the IV Corps across the river and in the direction of Lublin, to support the advance of Fourteenth Army on that city and its junction with Army Group North. The XIV Corps would remain west of the Vistula temporarily, and clear the area of Polish remnants still trying to escape across the river.

Polish planes bombed by the German air force.

On 13th September Tenth Army was given control over the VII and VIII Corps on the left flank of Fourteenth Army. The two corps were directed to continue their advance eastward, enveloping the Polish force at Bilgoraj and supporting the movement of Fourteenth Army on Lublin. This shift gave Tenth Army control over all German forces moving on Lublin from the west.

The IV Corps in the center of the Tenth Army front was across the Vistula on 14th September and moving east on a small Polish force at Krasnik. The city of Krasnik was taken on 15th September, and the corps moved rapidly past Lublin toward the Wieprz River. The XIV Corps concentrated on the west bank of the Vistula but did not cross in force, since some of its units were still occupied in clearing the area east of Radom of Polish remnants. On the Tenth Army right, the VII and VIII Corps attached from Fourteenth Army fought hard to destroy the Polish forces at Bilgoraj.

On 15th September Tenth Army reassumed control over the XI and XVI Corps that had been attached temporarily to Eighth Army, and Tenth Army became responsible for two fronts, one facing north toward Warsaw and the other east toward Lublin. The two corps on the Warsaw front would lay siege to the Polish capital from the south and move Panzer units between Warsaw and the Polish forces at Kutno, in support of the Eighth Army effort against the encircled western Polish armies. This would also provide flank protection for Tenth Army on the left, originally the mission of Eighth Army, and would free Eighth Army to concentrate on reducing the Polish force within the encirclement.

Tenth Army units on the Warsaw front held an east-west line. One infantry division was assigned to hold the southern approaches to the city, while the army concentrated stronger forces to move between Warsaw and the mass of Polish units at Kutno. The army commander directed the XI Corps to establish a bridgehead west of the Bzura River, to enable the XVI Corps to cross with its armour and attack the Poles from the east. This operation was worked out in close coordination with Eighth Army, pressing in on the Poles from the northwest, west, and southwest.

The bridgehead across the Bzura was established by 16 September, and the two Panzer divisions of XVI Corps prepared to attack immediately, with strong infantry support. A sharp spoiling attack by the encircled Polish force, in an attempt to break out to the east, prevented the implementation of this plan. Two infantry divisions were diverted to stem the attack, and a Panzer division was shifted northward to interpose itself between the Polish force and the capital. The disruption of the German plan mattered little, however, as the Polish force at Kutno expended its strength in attempts to break through the German encirclement.

Tenth Army was still committed against the eastern side of the Kutno encirclement as the Eighth Army and Luftwaffe launched a concerted attack the following day. The Polish units that escaped in the course of this action, most of them from the Poznan Army, were caught between the Vistula and Tenth Army units west of Warsaw. Twelve thousand prisoners were taken and Tenth Army moved on the Vistula to close the gap between Kutno and Warsaw.

On Tenth Army's eastern front, meanwhile, Bilgoraj was taken though stiff fighting continued southeast of the city, and Lublin was entered on 17th September. Advance units, passing between Polish concentrations to the north and south, reached the Wieprz River the same day. Tenth Army units were moving on Chelm and street fighting raged in Lublin as the second phase of Army Group South's operations came to a close. Tenth Army moved its headquarters to a point a short distance southwest of Warsaw and continued its drive in the direction of the Bug River, which would form the limiting line for its advance.

Fourteenth Army

On 10th September the XVII and XVIII Corps on the Fourteenth Army right crossed the San north and south of Przemysl, forced the 24th Infantry Division of the Polish general reserve to withdraw eastward and drove elements of the Cracow Army's 11th Infantry Division into the fortress city. The two German corps moved rapidly in the direction of Lwow, where the Polish High Command had established headquarters a few days before in an attempt to rally the withdrawing Polish Army for a stand in the southeastern part of the country. A task force under Colonel (later Field Marshal) Schoerner of the XVIII Corps' 1st Mountain Division reached the fortifications of the city on 12th September, and met spirited resistance from the garrison of 12,000 men. The mountain division quickly invested Lwow from the north and west, and cut all contact with the Polish force at Przemysl.

The city of Lwow is dominated by the Zboiska Heights to the north and northeast. It was important that these heights be seized without delay and that the exits from the city to the south and southeast be closed. Security would have to be provided against attacks from the west by the Polish force in Przemysl, and from the southwest, where the entire right flank of the division was exposed to Polish forces being moved up from the southeastern region of the country.

The attack to secure the ridges north and northeast of the city was launched by Group Schoerner at 10:00 on 13th September. The task force made rapid progress from the start, reaching the commanding height known as Hill 374 in the afternoon, and Zboiska and the surrounding ridges by dark. The major road to the north was cut by the capture of Zboiska, and the mountain troops dug in to hold their gains against a series of heavy Polish attacks. Other task forces moved out to secure the approaches from the southwest and Przemysl, and to close off exits from the city to the south and southeast.

On the left flank of Fourteenth Army, meanwhile, progress was slow, and VIII Corps, had to be shifted to clear the north bank of the Vistula as far as the junction with the San. The units opposing the forces on the left of the Fourteenth Army front comprised remnants of the Polish 21st and 22nd Mountain Divisions and the Rzeszow Armoured Calvary Brigade. The Polish units fought a strong rear guard action and withdrew across the San in a northeasterly direction to the dense forest and swamp area about Bilgoraj.

On 13th September Army Group South directed Fourteenth Army to send the remainder of its XVIII Corps to take Lwow, after which the corps was to move northward. The XVII and XXII Corps in the center of the Fourteenth Army line were to move to the northeast in the direction of Wlodzimierz and Hrubieszow, to effect a junction with Army Group North east of the Bug River. The VII and VIII Corps on the left were attached to Tenth Army, freeing Fourteenth Army for its extensive operations deeper into southeastern Poland. Army Headquarters moved to Rzeszow.

Lwow was completely encircled by XVIII Corps units by 14th September. Further west the Poles in Przemysl continued a stubborn resistance. Elements of several divisions had to be relieved from other missions for the assault on Przemysl's defences.

Przemysl fell on 15th September, marking the end of organized Polish resistance on the Fourteenth Army front except at Lwow, in the area northwest of Lwow, and near Bilgoraj. The protracted resistance at Lwow led the Fourteenth Army to direct the XXII Corps, after the capture of Wlodzimierz and Hrubieszow, to execute a move to the south with Panzer and motorized units with the mission of destroying the Polish forces still attempting to reach the fortress city. Detachments were also sent to the east to secure the oil fields below Lwow and prevent the escape of more Polish units and small parties to Romania. Meanwhile, a desperate attempt by Polish remnants to reach the garrison at Lwow was thwarted, at the expense of heavy casualties to the 1st Mountain Division, which held the XVIII Corps line north of the city and bore the brunt of the Polish attacks.

Fourteenth Army reported some local engagements on 16th September as isolated Polish units were encountered on the army front and in the rear areas. Heavy fighting continued at Lwow and in the area of Bilgoraj.

The intervention of the Red Army on 1th7 September made necessary some changes in the plan of operations. Fourteenth Army was ordered to advance no further than the line Stryj-Lwow-Bug River. The siege of Lwow would continue, temporarily ,and the oil-producing area south of Lwow was to be secured.

The meeting of German and Soviet forces in Poland was a cynical exercise in diplomacy between Molotov and von Ribbentrop.

CHAPTER 9

The End of the Campaign

The third and final phase of German operations in Poland consisted of (1) capturing the capital and other key fortress areas left behind the advancing Wehrmacht, and (2) evacuating eastern Poland ahead of the Red Army on the schedule ordered by Hitler. The capture of Warsaw, Modlin, and the port areas in The Corridor were only a matter of time as additional German infantry, artillery, and air forces became available with the approaching end of hostilities. Hitler's order for the evacuation of the area that was to be occupied by the Russians posed a more difficult problem, since German forces east of the Vistula and San Rivers were still engaged with remnants of the Polish Army at a number of points.

General

The Polish President and Marshal Rydz-Smigly had fled to Romania. A few organized Polish units still remained in the more inaccessible areas of eastern Poland, while other Polish troops had banded together under strong individual leaders regardless of rank. Units of both categories presented the Wehrmacht with a problem in discontinuing operations and withdrawing westward.

While these events were taking place, OKH was faced with the problem of shifting ground troops to the Westwall to meet a possible French and British attack. Divisions and higher commands were transferred from the Polish theater to the west as soon as they could be spared. As a result, the commands left behind had to assume the task of controlling vast areas and suppressing such scattered resistance as remained.

The battles for Warsaw and Modlin: early surrender overtures

Warsaw had come under siege with the approach of Third Army to the suburb of Praga, and OKH ordered a leaflet drop proposing negotiations with the Polish garrison for the evacuation of the city's civilian population and the diplomatic colony. A temporary cease-fire was arranged in the Praga sector while a German emissary from Third Army spoke with the Poles under a flag of truce on the morning of 16th September. The Polish commander refused to receive the German representative, nor would he accept a letter calling upon him to surrender. Another leaflet drop was made over the Polish capital in the afternoon of the same day, giving the population a cease-fire guarantee and 12 hours to evacuate the city. Third Army, however, suddenly resumed its shelling of Warsaw, returning the fire of the Polish batteries that either had not received or not heeded the German offer of a 12-hour truce. The barrage was finally stopped late that night, but little could be done to repair the damage to the German propaganda effort.

On 17th September the Poles broadcast a request that they be allowed to send representatives to arrange the removal of noncombatants. The request was acknowledged by the Germans, who indicated their willingness to receive the Polish emissaries, although Hitler had indicated that the time allotted for evacuation had elapsed. The Polish emissaries never appeared, however.

Initial German attacks

On 18th September OKH directed the resumption of operations against Warsaw, and Third and Tenth Armies commenced a heavy and sustained artillery bombardment of the Polish capital. The First Air Force joined the attack with a dive-bomber attack on water works and other utilities on 20 September. On the ground small task forces made a series of probing attacks against the city's defences.

Officer prisoners revealed that the garrison of Warsaw was composed in large part of regular troops, under General Rommel, former commander of the Lodz Army. Morale was good, under the circumstances, and ammunition in ample supply. The city's communications system and sources of electric power were still intact. The food situation was unknown, but at best it could only be fair in view of the large civilian population to be fed and the impossibility of any resupply from outside Warsaw. Third Army met spirited resistance to the north and east of the city, as did Tenth Army to the south and west.

A battered and bombed Polish airfield viewed from the skies.

Progress was slow in reducing the city of Warsaw by artillery fire and air bombardment. The garrison had made good use of the brief cease-fires to build additional barricades and weapons emplacements, and Warsaw's artillery still answered the fire of the Germans. A large militia force, hastily organized, supplemented the efforts of the Army and police. The situation with the diplomatic colony was resolved on 21st September when it was arranged for personnel of the neutral embassies, consulates, and missions to leave the city through the Third Army lines.

Hitler visited Third Army units on 22nd September and observed the shelling of Praga from a church tower outside the city. The Führer was opposed to an assault on that part of the city east of the Vistula. However, he approved an attack on that part of Warsaw west of the Vistula that would be occupied by the Germans according to the German-Soviet pact. An attack from the west would also drive the mass of the Warsaw population out of the city to the east and relieve the Germans of responsibility for them. Hitler was informed the same day of the death of General von Fritsch, whom he had removed as commander in chief of the Army over a year earlier. General von Fritsch, despite his retired status, had insisted on his prerogative as honorary regimental commander of accompanying the 12th Artillery Regiment of the 12th Infantry Division into the field, and was killed while observing a division action before Praga.

The Eighth Army attack

Various plans to take that part of Warsaw west of the Vistula were discussed and discarded. It was finally decided by OKH that Army Group South's Eighth Army, which had finished clearing Kutno, would direct the effort to capture Warsaw. Eighth Army headquarters moved to a point southwest of the capital on 24th September, relieving Tenth Army Headquarters, which moved southward to the vicinity of Kielce again. Eighth Army quickly completed its plans and final dispositions for the attack.

The Eighth Army Commander, General Blaskowitz, was instructed that he was not to permit the civilian population to leave the city prior to the assault. The worsening food situation within Warsaw and the large numbers to be fed would aid materially in hastening the surrender of the capital.

The Eighth Army attack began on 26th September, with a heavy air and artillery bombardment followed by an assault from the south. The first and second line of bunkers were taken, and prisoners reported that communications within the city had been cut and electric power was no longer available. Third Army supported the attack by a heavy artillery barrage on Warsaw's defences from the north. By order of Hitler, the capture of the city was to be accomplished by 3rd October, before the arrival of the Russians at Praga to the east of the Vistula.

Two Polish envoys crossed the German lines north of Warsaw the evening of 26th September with a letter from General Rommel requesting a 24-hour cessation of fire and a surrender parley. The cease-fire request was refused and the German artillery fire intensified, though the Poles were informed that a local truce could be arranged in order to allow Polish emissaries to cross the lines in the event General Rommel decided to surrender the city. The incident was reported through army and army group headquarters to OKH, which directed that the surrender would be taken by Eighth Army and that only an unconditional surrender would be accepted.

General Kutrzeba appeared the following morning to accept the German terms in the name of General Rommel. The Polish envoy was immediately conducted to Eighth Army to conclude the negotiations for the surrender. Hostilities ceased at 14:00 on 27th September, and 140,000 Polish troops lay down their arms, including the garrison in the eastern suburb of Praga. All Polish military personnel were ordered to be ready for evacuation by 29th September. Warsaw was in a serious situation, with over 16,000 of the garrison wounded and heavy casualties among the civilian population. The supply of drinking water had been cut off for five days, making it necessary for the garrison and population to use the water of the Vistula; an epidemic of typhoid appeared imminent. All public utilities had been heavily damaged and would require extensive repairs. The city was also on the verge of starvation.

The capture of Modlin

Modlin continued to resist despite the surrender of the capital and a series of heavy attacks by the Third Army, supported by Eighth Army south of the city. The cessation of hostilities at Warsaw made large masses of artillery and increased air support available to Third Army. The bombardment of the fortress city was intensified and German infantry managed to infiltrate the first line of fortifications. An armistice was arranged at 07:30 on 28th September and the formal surrender to Third Army's II Corps took place the following day. Twenty-four thousand Polish troops at Modlin laid down their arms in unconditional surrender, and German troops entered the fortress at noon. General Thommee, commander of the Modlin force, attributed his surrender to the cutting off of the water supply; the loss of food stores in the bombardment; the complete exhaustion of the defending troops, who had suffered 4,000 casualties in wounded alone; and the infantry attack.

Operations in the northern area of The Corridor became a separate campaign following the junction of the German Third and Fourth Armies. The German effort to capture the Polish port areas continued throughout all three phases of operations by Army Groups North and South, and ended only a few days before the destruction of the last organized Polish force in the field.

The 207th Infantry Division of the I Frontier Guard Corps linked with units of Brigade Eberhard from Danzig to present a front to the Poles in the Gdynia-Wejherowo (Neustadt) area as it turned north in the upper Corridor. Brigade Eberhard was placed under operational control of I Frontier Guard Corps, and the entire command was redesignated Corps Kaupisch. Steady progress against scattered resistance was reported until 6th September, when the advancing German units began to encounter Polish naval forces committed in a ground combat role.

The major Polish unit in line was identified as a naval infantry brigade, organized by expansion of the naval infantry battalions in Wejherowo and Gdynia to the status of regiments. The naval brigade and a number of miscellaneous units were under the command of a Colonel Dabek.

Bombs striking the fortress of Modlin.

Wejherowo fell on 9th September, and a tight German ring was drawn about Gdynia and the coastal area immediately to the north, known as the Oksywie (Oxhoefter) Flats. Corps Kaupisch made another important gain on 9th September when a frontier guard regiment captured the port of Puck (Putzig) to the north of Gdynia and cut the main rail line to the naval base at Hela.

Corps Kaupisch encountered heavy resistance on 10th and 11th September as it moved in on Gdynia from its three land sides. From the Danzig area Brigade Eberhard pushed north along the coast, linked on its left with the 207th Infantry Division, which made its attack from the west. The northern side of the German encirclement was held by a frontier guard regiment, which rested its left flank on the sea and had contact with the regiment that had taken Puck.

The Polish force at Hela was completely cut off from land contact with the mainland on 12th September, when the frontier guard regiment at Puck sent a strong force to the north and reached the coast. That night the Poles at Gdynia launched an attack at the boundary line between the 207th Infantry Division and Brigade Eberhard, regained some ground, and temporarily disrupted the schedule of the German advance.

The German line was restored the following day, and on 14th September Gdynia was taken. The Polish force of Colonel Dabek was forced to retreat to the Oksywie Flats, under a steady artillery and air bombardment. The Schleswig-Holstein, lying offshore, joined the artillery bombardment the following day, and an attack by Stuka dive bombers destroyed a major ammunition depot established on the Flats by the Poles. That same day Corps Kaupisch passed to the control of the newly established Military Government Command Danzig-West Prussia.

The German shelling of the Flats and a series of heavy air attacks continued through 16th and 17th September. A total of 2,000 prisoners were taken on 18 September, and the German attack of 19th September became a clearing operation. Oksywie was taken in the late afternoon and the Germans had established firm control of the Flats by evening. Colonel Dabek committed suicide rather than surrender his command.

The destruction of the Gdynia force completed German operations in the upper Corridor, except for Hela. A regimental combat team of the 207th Infantry Division, reinforced by all but one battalion of the division artillery and by the artillery of Brigade Eberhard, was assigned the task of taking Hela. The extremely narrow peninsula extending out to the Polish naval base precluded the commitment of a force of any greater size, and a seaborne landing against heavily fortified Hela promised little success without heavy losses.

The regiment assigned to take Hela made a limited advance out onto the peninsula on 21st September, to find it heavily mined and stubbornly defended. Hela was taken under fire by the Schleswig-Holstein, which was joined by the Schlesien on 24th September. The rail line used by the Poles to move their heavy artillery out to positions on the peninsula was cut by Stuka bombing on 25th September and the offshore bombardment intensified. On 27th September air support was withdrawn as the Luftwaffe was deployed to the west. With the support of the two old battleships, another ground attack was launched down the narrow peninsula on 29th September. A further attack on 30 September gained the tiny village of Ceynowa for the Germans, and a final assault was planned for 2nd October.

A final German attack was not necessary. On 1st October Rear Admiral J. Unrug, commander at Hela, requested a surrender parley. The Polish emissary accepted the German

A ruined suburb of Warsaw demonstrates the destructive potential of the Luftwaffe.

terms of unconditional surrender at 17:00 the same day and all resistance ceased. A total of 5,000 prisoners were taken at Hela to bring the number captured by Corps Kaupisch during the course of operations to 18,000. Hela also yielded 41 artillery pieces of various calibers and two small naval vessels.

The Evacuation of eastern Poland

Hitler's order to withdraw to the demarcation line of the Narew-Vistula-San Rivers was communicated to the army groups on 20th September and necessitated a move far to the west of the line of 17th September. The Führer's directive required immediate disengagement from the Polish forces still carrying on hostilities and withdrawal without delay to the west of the line formed by the three rivers.

The order for evacuation took little cognizance of the military situation. The German combat units in eastern Poland had several thousand wounded they had been unable to evacuate, thousands of prisoners of war, a large number of disabled tanks and other vehicles, and in addition they were in possession of large stocks of Polish Army matériel, ammunition, foodstuffs, and other supplies. Personnel, vehicles, and animals had just completed a campaign over vast distances; the men and horses required rest and the motor vehicles were in need of repairs. Rail transportation to move any but a small portion of the German forces to the west was completely inadequate.

To effect the withdrawal in orderly fashion, the German ground forces on 21st September were ordered by OKH to draw back along a series of phase lines, each located progressively farther to the west. Where possible, an interval of 15 miles was to be maintained between the Wehrmacht and the Red Army, but unit commanders were authorized to deal with the Russians should they overtake German troops on the move. The wounded were to be left

Warsaw burning from aerial bombardment.

behind with medical personnel for later evacuation. Captured matériel was to be evacuated by the Germans where practicable, otherwise it would be left behind for the Russians. German matériel that could not be evacuated was to be left under guard and removed later. Particular care was to be taken to destroy disabled Mark IV tanks that could not be salvaged.

Negotiations with the Red Army during the evacuation were often to prove exasperating to German commanders. Despite the offers of the Soviet Government and Red Army commanders to give armed support to German units still engaged with the remnants of the Polish Army, the Russians procrastinated about active assistance in most cases until the Germans no longer needed it. The problem of identification was also to plague German commanders. The Red Army and Polish Army uniforms were somewhat similar, and German units not infrequently mistook one for the other.

The civilian population that had fled eastward at the approach of the Germans was also to become a problem during the evacuation of eastern Poland. Fearful of the Russians, the mass of refugees that had fled into eastern Poland before the Germans turned about and moved westward again, clogging the already inadequate road system and blocking military traffic.

The Army Group North area

The XIX Corps turned Brzesc over to the Red Army on 22nd September in a formal ceremony in which both German and Russian units paraded. The corps then began its return to East Prussia, where tanks and other motor vehicles could receive urgently needed repairs and maintenance.

On 23rd September units of the 10th Panzer Division engaged in a sharp skirmish with advancing Russian cavalry. Russian losses were reported as two dead and 23 wounded. The incident was attributed to a mistake in identification and was settled by the local German and Russian commanders. A number of other localities were turned over to the control of the Red Army without incident.

General von Bock commented at some length on the impression made by the Russians. The Army Group North commander noted that the Red Army was poorly disciplined and the troops were unsoldierly in appearance. The political commissar were truculent and unfriendly. Bock directed that contact would be maintained only through officers and that there would be no general fraternization.

The evacuation in the Army Group North area was almost completed by the time Warsaw surrendered. Only a few German units remained east of the demarcation line, hunting down Polish units or safeguarding installations of military importance until the arrival of the Russians. The XXI Corps, with one division and a number of security units, maintained contact with the Russians in the north of the army group area. In the southern part of the army group area contact was maintained by units of I Corps near Warsaw.

The headquarters of Army Group North and Fourth Army returned to East Prussia preparatory to movement to the west, and on 2nd October the area of responsibility of Army Group North was transferred to Third Army in a formal ceremony. Third Army promptly set about securing the northern Polish areas under German control.

The Army Group South area

Rundstedt reported the destruction of the Polish concentrations south of Bilgoraj during the several days preceding the receipt of orders to evacuate eastern Poland. Fourteenth Army on 20th September also reported the capture of 11,000 prisoners northwest of Lwow, ending operations in that area. The siege of Lwow was still in progress when Army Group South received orders to withdraw west of the Vistula-San River line.

The evacuation order instructed Rundstedt to leave the reduction of Lwow to the

A Polish bunker lies destroyed as the German infantry arrive to survey the conquest.

Russians. The attack planned by XVIII Corps for 21st September was cancelled, and the corps prepared to move to the west. Contact had already been established with the Russians when Red Army tanks had suddenly appeared at Winniki, southeast of Lwow.

The Polish garrison of Lwow abruptly and unexpectedly surrendered to the 1st Mountain Division as it made ready to withdraw from its siege lines on 21st September. The occupation of the city was left to the Russians and the 1st Mountain Division moved westward toward the San with the rest of the XVIII Corps.

Tenth Army ceased operations at Chelm and began its withdrawal to the west of the demarcation line. Chelm had already been taken under artillery fire and preparations were under way for an infantry assault when the withdrawal order arrived.

A heavy engagement was reported in the Tenth Army area on 23rd September, when a strong Polish force attacked the withdrawing Germans in the Zamosc region. Tenth Army reacted quickly, surrounding part of the Polish force southwest of Zamosc and driving the remainder to the south and into the area to be occupied by the Red Army.

By 30th September Eighth Army was engaged in evacuating the Polish garrison of Warsaw and with the numerous tasks involved in establishing control over the Polish capital. Tenth Army was still in contact with Polish remnants east of the Vistula, and Fourteenth Army had completed its evacuation to the San River.

Several incidents occurred during this period in the Fourteenth Army area when German and Russian troops exchanged fire. The incidents were settled by the local commanders concerned and no further action was taken by either side.

On 1st October Tenth Army was alerted for redeployment back to Germany. At the same time, OKH informed Army Group South that the demarcation line had been changed again and would follow the Pisia and Narew Eivers to Ostroleka, thence past Ostrow Mazowiecka to the Bug, south along the latter to a point east of Tomaszow, west to the San, and south to the Slovak frontier. This would extend the German zone to the east, in places over 100 miles. The change had been made at the request of the Soviet Government, which desired to add Lithuania to its own sphere of influence. In exchange for Lithuania the Russians were willing to give the Germans that area of Poland between Warsaw and the Bug River.

Army Group South's commander was redesignated OB EAST (Oberbefehlshaber Ost) as of 3rd October, with responsibility for all of occupied Poland. Under this reorganization, Rundstedt became the Commander in Chief East.

The Polish defenders on the Hel peninsula on the shore of the Baltic Sea held out until 2nd October. The last organized stand by the Polish Army was made at Kock, where the last operational unit of the Polish Army, General Franciszek Kleeberg's Samodzielna Grupa Operacyjna "Polesie", continued to resist and heavy fighting raged from 4th to 6th October. Panzer and motorized infantry units of Tenth Army ended this last Polish resistance, and the Kock force surrendered on 6th October, adding 17,000 more to the total of prisoners taken by the Germans. The Polish Campaign was over, though sporadic fighting was to continue in some of the more remote areas for a considerable period.

Despite a Polish victory at the Battle of Szack, after which the Soviets notoriously executed all the officers and NCOs they had captured, the Red Army reached the line of rivers Narew, Western Bug, Vistula and San by September 28, in many cases they met German units advancing from the other direction.

Results of the Campaign

The German Army suffered a total of 8,082 officers and men killed, 27,278 wounded, and 5,029 missing in its 36 days of operations in Poland. Luftwaffe and Navy losses were much lighter. The figure on missing Army personnel can be considered as high, in view of the fact that the German Army destroyed the Polish Army and recovered most prisoners taken by organized military units.

Two hundred and seventeen tanks were destroyed during the period 1st -30th September, including 89 Mark I vehicles, 83 Mark II's, 26 Mark III's, and 19 Mark IV's. Neutral sources also reported over 400 German aircraft of all types destroyed. Sustained operations over poor roads and rough terrain far ahead of maintenance facilities was extremely wearing on armoured vehicles as well as trucks, requiring extensive repair work at the end of the campaign. German aircraft that participated in the campaign were in little better condition by the end of operations, having had to fly repeated sorties as the weather permitted, often from bases with only the most primitive landing and few if any maintenance facilities. The situation in the XIX Corps perhaps best exemplified the material situation by the end of operations when the entire corps was temporarily immobilized in East Prussia while its tanks, armoured cars, and trucks were overhauled and repaired.

The Polish losses were staggering. The Germans claimed 694,000 prisoners of war, out of some 800,000 who had served in Poland's defence; the remainder were killed, captured by the Russians, had fled into Romania or Hungary, or had hidden in isolated areas of their own country. The Germans, by their own count, captured a total of 3,214 field pieces, 16,500 machine guns, 1,700 mortars, and enormous quantities of small arms and ammunition.8-16 The captured ordnance and other matériel was not considered suitable for issue by Wehrmacht standards, but could be put to use by Germany's various satellites.

The civilian population which came under German control as a result of the campaign comprised approximately 22 million persons. Some three-quarters of a million were ethnic Germans and available for military service. Some of the other minorities, as the Ukrainians, were not opposed to cooperation and service with the Germans. However, the bulk of the Polish population under German control were considered as the people of an occupied country. As a result, sizeable military forces had to be maintained in Poland until the time that the Wehrmacht began to concentrate its forces in the east for the campaign against the Soviet Union more than a year later. The units assigned to this occupation duty were usually of far lower combat potential than those assigned to front-line service, but the necessity of keeping a military force in Poland at all tied down personnel and equipment that might have been put to use elsewhere in the major war effort in which the Reich now found itself engaged.

CHAPTER 10

The Intervention of the Soviet Union

The rapid progress of the German armies by 3rd September prompted Foreign Minister Ribbentrop to dispatch a cable to Moscow, suggesting the movement of Red Army troops into eastern Poland. Molotov's reply was equivocal, stating that the Soviet Government felt the time not yet proper. However, the Soviet Foreign Minister committed his government to intervention at a time when it would be advantageous to the Soviet Union and to Germany.

Diplomatic negotiations

Ribbentrop dispatched a second cable on the matter of intervention on 9 September, calling attention to the fact that the Soviet military attaché had been recalled to Moscow. Molotov's reply promised military action within the next few days. The Soviet Foreign Minister also admitted that the summoning of the military attaché to Moscow had been prompted by the impending movement of the Red Army into Poland.

Frontline positions near Modlin

The destroyed remains of the Polish Army.

The German Ambassador in Moscow dispatched two additional cables to Berlin on 9th and 10th September. According to the German Ambassador, Molotov had promised more than the Red Army could accomplish within the span of a few days. The Soviet Government had been surprised by the speed of the German advance, and Red Army preparations' for a movement on the scale required were still far from complete. Three million men had been mobilized, but some logistical arrangements still had to be made. Schools were being transformed into temporary hospitals, the supply of gasoline for nonmilitary uses had been curtailed, and certain foodstuffs had already disappeared from the open market.

The cables further indicated that Molotov was desirous of minimizing the odium attached to an aggressive move into eastern Poland. Thus the Russians would announce that the Red Army was coming to the aid of the Ukrainians and Byelorussians (White Russians) resident in eastern Poland who were threatened by the advancing Germans. The Soviet Union was also concerned about a recent announcement by General von Brauchitsch that had been interpreted as an indication that a Polish-German armistice was imminent.

Ribbentrop assured the Soviet Foreign Minister on 13th September that the Brauchitsch statement referred only to the disputed Corridor and other areas adjoining the Reich where organized Polish resistance had ceased. Meanwhile, German forces had advanced to and beyond the Narew-Vistula-San River line and forced the mass of the Polish armies into the encirclements at Kutno and Radom.

On 14th September Ribbentrop was informed that Soviet preparations were complete and a movement into eastern Poland could be expected shortly. However, the Soviet Government refused to order the Red Army to move until the Polish capital had been taken, and requested that the German Government estimate the date by which the capture of Warsaw might be accomplished.

Ribbentrop's reply of the following day, 15th September, contained a note of urgency. The German Foreign Minister stated that the fall of the Polish capital was a matter of only a few days. He urged an immediate move by the Russians, to prevent eastern Poland becoming a political vacuum or the population forming one or more small states. Ribbentrop further proposed the issuance of a joint communique to the effect that Germany and the Soviet Union were moving into Poland to restore peace and order in an area of interest to the Reich and the Soviet state. This would make unnecessary the announcement that the Russians were intervening in Poland in behalf of Russian minorities threatened by the Germans. Ribbentrop ended his cable with a request that the Soviet Government set a date and hour for the movement of troops across the Polish-Russian frontier.

Molotov's answer of 16th September promised military action the next day or the day following; Stalin was in conference with military leaders and would give the date and time that night. At 02:00 on 17th September, in the presence of Molotov, the German Ambassador was informed by Stalin that Soviet troops would move into Poland at 06:00 that same day. Stalin requested that German aircraft remain west of the line Bialystok-Brzesc-Lwow, since Russian aircraft would begin bombing operations in the area of Lwow immediately following the crossing of the frontier. Stalin closed the interview with the request that all military matters henceforth be conducted between Marshal Voroshilov for the Red Army and Generalleutnant Ernst Koestring, Germany Military Attaché in Moscow.

From available records it appears that the German Foreign Minister and other government leaders had not taken the military officers directing operations into their confidence on the negotiations being carried on between Berlin and Moscow. Jodl mentioned later that he was informed of the impending move by the Red Army only two or three days before it took place. Warlimont, chief operations officer of Jodl's Armed Forces Operations Office, states that he knew nothing of the move until called by General Koestring from Moscow the morning the Red Army crossed the frontier. Koestring himself had not been fully advised of the Red Army's preparations and plans to cross into Poland. As a result of this lack of direction from the Reich's highest official quarters, which were themselves completely uninformed of the actual Russian intentions until less than four hours before the actual intervention of the Soviet Union, German troops continued to move eastward and beyond the demarcation line which had been agreed upon. Some German units could not disengage from contact with the Poles immediately upon receipt of orders to do so; others were forced to fight a series of rear guard actions as they moved back to the demarcation line.

The joint communique issued on 18th September stated only that the Russian movement into Poland did not conflict with the nonaggression pact and that both German and Soviet Governments desired only to restore order and assist the Poles to reestablish their political existence. Two days later the Soviet Government proposed that no residual Polish Government be formed and that the country be partitioned along the line formed by the Soviet and German spheres of influence agreed upon in the nonaggression pact. The Reich

Fortress 9 of the Warsaw defences is captured by the German army.

Government immediately assented and Ribbentrop prepared to go to Moscow to conclude negotiations and settle the fate of the Polish state.

The Red Army's intervention forces

The stipulation that a wide interval would be maintained between the withdrawing Germans and the advancing Russians made it difficult to obtain precise information about the size or composition of the Red Army force that entered eastern Poland. German military reports of the first few days make reference only to "Russian units." Repeated contacts where one force met the other, as at Brzesc and Lwow, soon gave the Germans a somewhat clearer picture of the Russian military situation.

The Red Army crossed the border into eastern Poland with two army groups, called "fronts" in Soviet usage. It was of particular interest to the Germans to note that the units of these two fronts were drawn from the interior of the Soviet Union. Garrison troops in the frontier areas remained at their home stations, and the defensive capability of the Red Army in the western Soviet Union was not greatly weakened by the venture into Poland.

The White Russian Front, in the north, was commanded by Army Commander Kovalev, with headquarters in Minsk. (The regular ranks for general officers, except for marshals, had not yet been reintroduced in the Red Army.) The front consisted of the Third and Eleventh Armies, the former assigned the mission of advancing on Brzesc and Bialystok while the latter moved into the area of Poland adjacent to the Lithuanian and East Prussian frontiers. The Third Army comprised one. tank, one cavalry, and one infantry corps, with a total of two infantry and three cavalry divisions and an unknown number of tank brigades. The Eleventh

Army controlled three similar corps, with one additional infantry division.

The Ukrainian Front, on the south, was commanded by Army Commander Timoshenko, with headquarters at Proskurov, east of Lwow. The front consisted of the First and Tenth Armies, the former assigned the mission of moving on Lwow while the latter advanced on the Lublin area. The First Army was the far stronger of the two, with a tank corps, two cavalry corps, and four infantry corps. First Army had a total of at least six infantry and six cavalry divisions, and an undetermined number of tank brigades. The Tenth Army comprised only two corps, with two cavalry divisions and an undetermined number of infantry divisions.

According to the estimates made at OKW, the Russians committed a total of at least 20 to 24 infantry divisions, 15 cavalry divisions, and nine tank brigades to the advance into Poland. No figures were given on the number of troops that this may have involved. Since they expected to meet little or no resistance and possibly in order to impress the Poles and Germans, the Russians sent their tank and motorized units on ahead, where the terrain permitted, followed by the infantry at some interval. Horse cavalry units were used in broken country or areas in which the road net did not permit the use of motor vehicles. This accounts for the frequent mention in German headquarters journals of the sudden appearance of Russian armoured and horse cavalry units.

The actions of the Russians on moving into Poland put the lie to their claims of assistance to the Russian minorities. The Red Army offered the Germans armed assistance wherever it should be necessary, even though this assistance usually came too late, and destroyed or captured organized Polish forces with which it came into contact even prior to the surrender of Warsaw and the destruction of the last major Polish force at Kock. Little information as to Russian activities in eastern Poland was allowed to leak out once the Red Army established control of the area; no mention at all of these activities appears in German reports of the period, possibly due in some part to lack of interest in areas beyond the control of the Wehrmacht and in which the Reich had no immediate concern, but more likely because of the stringent security measures taken by the Russians in their newly acquired territories.

CHAPTER 11

The Fourth Partition and German Occupation of Poland

Three military government commands, responsible directly to OKH, followed the German armies into Poland. These commands had army status, and were placed in control of the three military government areas (Militaerbezirke) into which western Poland was arbitrarily divided; headquarters were at Danzig, Poznan, and Cracow. The officers in charge of these commands were known as military government commanders (Militaerbefehlshaber), and their mission during the period of operations consisted chiefly of securing the German counterpart to the United States Army's communications zone, from the border of the Reich to the rear areas of the field armies. To carry out their mission, the military government commands were assigned one or two third — or fourth wave divisions, some frontier guard units that had crossed the border with the Army, and a number of security battalions consisting of troops of the older age groups.

The command at Poznan was the first to take control of its assigned area, moving in 11th September, under General der Artillerie Alfred von Vollard-Bockelberg. The second, at Danzig and responsible for the former German province of West Prussia, moved in the following day, under General der Artillerie Walter Heitz. The third, at Cracow, was commanded by General List of the Fourteenth Army, functioning in a dual role, and assisted by a small additional staff. This last command became operational on 13th September.

By 25th September the end of the campaign was fast approaching and Hitler ordered the establishment of a military government organization for the occupied Polish territories. This organization would include four area military government commands, with headquarters at Poznan, Danzig, Cracow, and Lodz. The Führer selected Rundstedt as commander in chief for the conquered eastern territories, placing him in control of tactical units and military government. Army Group North and Fourth Army headquarters soon left for the west, to be followed shortly by Tenth Army. On its transition to OB EAST, Rundstedt's headquarters found itself in control of the four military government commands and the three armies remaining in Poland.

On 3rd October a change was also made in the tactical organization when three frontier army commands were established to secure the new frontier with the Soviet Union. Third Army, which had moved to Ortelsburg in East Prussia, was redesignated Frontier Army Command North; Eighth Army was redesignated Frontier Army Command Center, with its commander functioning concurrently as Military Government Commander Lodz; and Fourteenth Army was renamed Frontier Army Command South, with its commander becoming concurrently Military Government Commander Cracow. The three headquarters retained their army status but reference to them was made by their territorial designations.

West Prussia and the Poznan areas were annexed to Germany as Reichsgarue (administrative districts under the German Ministry of the Interior) on 8th October, the annexation to be effective as of 1st November. A small strip of Silesia taken by Poland after World War I was also annexed directly to Silesia. At the same time Wehrkreise XX and XXI were formed in the areas of the new Reichsgaue. The Military Government Command Danzig-West Prussia became the headquarters of Wehrkreis XX and the Military Government Command Poznan became Wehrkreis XXI. As Wehrkreise, these commands were transferred to the control of the Replacement and Training Army.

On 12th October Hitler directed the establishment of a government general under civilian control for the area of German-occupied Poland not annexed to the Reich. This was done to ensure the carrying out of Hitler's policy of ruthless destruction of the Polish nation, a task he was convinced the Army would not complete. As governor general he appointed Dr. Hans Frank, a lawyer and National Socialist Party figure, who had functioned as chief civilian administrator for Rundstedt. Frank would be responsible to Hitler, with Dr. Seyss-Inquart as his deputy. Hitler felt that he could depend on Frank to put his racial theories as expressed in Mein Kampf into practice. The government general, however, was not to become operational until such time as Hitler decreed the military government of Poland at an end.

Brauchitsch, through Keitel, brought the Army's protest against this reorganization to Hitler on 17th October. Hitler replied that the Army would be relieved of the administration of the occupied territories and remained firm in his decision to establish a civilian administration; his decision was made public by decree on 19th October 1939, when it was directed that as of 26th October the occupation of Poland would be directed by the government general of Dr. Frank. Headquarters OB EAST would be responsible only for security and the defence of Germany against any attack from that quarter.

Effective 26th October East Prussia (Wehrkreis I) was added to the command of OB EAST for defensive purposes and the commanding general of Frontier Army Command North became concurrently commanding general of Wehrkreis I. This realignment of forces gave OB EAST a solid front from the Baltic southward to Romania. In addition to the three frontier army commands, OKH assigned OB EAST the XXXI, XXXII, XXXIV, XXXV, and XXXVI Corps Commands, formed on 5th October 1939 from the frontier commands that had participated in the attack on Poland, with 12 third- and fourth-wave divisions, a cavalry brigade, and various security units.

The redeployment from Poland did not fill the requirement for combat-experienced commands and staffs for the direction of the campaign against France, which Hitler still hoped to launch before the end of the year. As a consequence, an exchange of headquarters became necessary. On 13th October the Fourteenth Army staff less the small group originally assigned to General List for the purpose of establishing a military government organization in southern Poland was replaced as headquarters of Frontier Army Command South by the staff of Army "A" (a provisional army formed to control units along the Netherlands frontier in September 1939) under General der Artillerie Alexander Ulex from the western front. The

Eighth Army staff on the same day was replaced by the Fifth Army staff of General der Infanterie Liebmann as headquarters of Frontier Army Command Center at Lodz. The next move was that of Rundsted's headquarters itself. The planning for the campaign in the west revealed the need for another army group headquarters. On 18th October Rundstedt and his former Army Group South headquarters (that had been temporarily designated OB EAST) began their move to the west.

General Blaskowitz was appointed to succeed Rundstedt on 19th October and Frontier Army Command Center headquarters was redesignated OB EAST. The organization of a new headquarters for the Frontier Army Command Center area was begun immediately, but by 30th October the needs of the western front were so pressing that it was decided to use the personnel and equipment collected for the formation of the Eighteenth Army headquarters in western Germany. As no further personnel were available to form a substitute staff, OB EAST had to assume a concurrent function as Frontier Army Command Center, effective 2nd November. By late October only one of the original army headquarters remained in the east—Third Army which was functioning as Frontier Army Command North. On 22nd October Third Army relinquished its responsibilities as Frontier Army Command North to Wehrkreis I and moved to the west to become the Sixteenth Army. The area of responsibility of Wehrkreis I was enlarged to include that area of Poland which had been the responsibility of Frontier Army Command North.

During the winter and early spring of 1940 the needs of the other fronts made further demands on OB EAST and a number of the corps commands and most of the third-wave divisions were withdrawn from Poland. The OB EAST (and Frontier Army Command Center) staff of Blaskowitz was moved to the west to become the nucleus of the new Ninth Army headquarters. Frontier Army Command South headquarters became OB EAST, with the XXXIV and XXXV Corps Commands and seven newly organized security divisions, while Wehrkreis I retained control of three new security divisions. This remained the OB EAST organization until the end of the French campaign, when Eighteenth Army and a number of corps and combat divisions could be transferred from France to the east.

CHAPTER 12

Conclusions

There are several common misconceptions regarding the Polish September Campaign perhaps the most wide spread of these is the hoary old tale that the Polish Army was so backward it attempted to fight tanks with horse-mounted cavalry wielding lances and swords.

General

Although it is true that in 1939 Poland still fielded eleven cavalry brigades and Polish military doctrine emphasized cavalry units as elite units. this was not unusual as other armies of that time including the rapidly modernizing German army nonetheless fielded and extensively used horse cavalry units. The Polish cavalry had been modernized was equipped with modern small arms and effective light artillery such as the Swedish Bofors 37 mm antitank gun. No Polish cavalry ever charged German tanks or even entrenched infantry. They usually acted as mobile infantry and were properly designated as reconnaissance units executed cavalry charges only in rare situations against broken enemy infantry. The myth appears to have originated from a German propaganda article concerning the Battle of Krojanty when Polish cavalry were surprised by hidden armoured vehicles and suffered heavy casualties.

The other wide spread myth is that the Polish air force was destroyed on the ground in the first day of the war. The truth is that Polish Air Force, though numerically inferior, had been moved from air bases to small camouflaged airfields shortly before the war. The losses on the first day were mainly old trainers and auxiliary aircraft. These were indeed destroyed on the ground. The Polish Air Force in fact remained active in the first two weeks of the campaign, inflicting serious damage on the Luftwaffe which amounted to around two hundred German planes which destroyed in aerial combat. Many skilled Polish pilots escaped afterwards to the United Kingdom and were deployed by the RAF during the Battle of Britain. Fighting from British bases, Polish pilots were on average the most successful in shooting down German aircraft.

The myth that Poland offered little resistance and surrendered quickly has also gained some currency. Germany in fact sustained relatively heavy losses, especially in vehicles and aircraft. the invasion Poland cost the Germans the equivalent of an entire armoured division and 25 percent of its air strength. As regards the duration, the September Campaign lasted only one week less than the Battle of France in 1940. The poles fought well when once considers how outnumbered they were. In May 1940 even though the Anglo-French forces were much closer to parity with the Germans in numerical strength and equipment. It is likely that the Polish Army which was in the process was preparing the Romanian

Bridgehead, would have prolonged it's resistance beyond that of the allied armies in France, however this plan was abandoned due to the Soviet invasion of Poland on September 17th, 1939. It should be noted that Poland also never officially surrendered to the Germans. With the country under German occupation, the Polish army continued to fight underground, as Armia Krajowa and forest partisans – LeÊni. The Polish resistance movement in World War II in German-occupied Poland was one of the largest resistance movements in all of occupied Europe.

In general, the Polish Campaign proved to be very challenging for the Germans. The Polish campaign demonstrated the speed and power possessed by the new Panzers and Panzer Divisions. It provided Germans with the first wide spread experience of using armour in combat conditions. The Germans also learned that tanks were not suited for combat in built up areas, this was brought home by the heavy losses suffered in Warsaw. They also discovered that well organized anti-tank defences are very dangerous. Polish Campaign also proved what they had suspected already that the Panzer Mark I and Mark II were no longer suitable to employed as frontline combat tanks and should be completely replaced as soon as possible with heavier Mark III and IV models. During the course of the campaign, Light Divisions proved to be unsuccessful being too weak to perform task of either regular infantry or motorized infantry.

The German campaign in Poland in 1939 has come to be regarded by many as little more than a manoeuvre for the new Wehrmacht. However, the casualty figures and losses in matériel for the period of combat show that the campaign was more than just an exercise with live ammunition. Rundstedt supported this view on operations in Poland in one of his rare commentaries following World War II. The bulk of the German armed forces had to be committed to overcome the Poles, and the expenditure in ammunition, gasoline, and matériel was such as to preclude concurrent German operations on a similar scale in the west or elsewhere.

The unrealistic impression of the campaign was heightened by the German propaganda effort that proceeded apace with operations in the field. The German armies were depicted as highly motorized, with tank support out of proportion to the actual number of armoured vehicles they had available, and with fleets of aircraft supporting ground units on short notice with maximum efficiency. Little mention was made of the horse drawn supply columns, of the infantry divisions which often force marched on foot at the rate of 30 miles per day.

Nonetheless the Wehrmacht was demonstrably a highly effective fighting organization and had accomplished much in putting the theory of mobile warfare to the test of battle. "Panzer" division and "Luftwaffe" soon became familiar terms. from the short Polish campaign it was obvious that the era of trench warfare had ended. Movement had been restored to the battlefield.

With the bulk of the German forces committed in Poland the opportunity for a successful attack against the Westwall presented itself, but the allies were incapable of offensive action and the chance had passed by the time the Polish Campaign ended. Hitler and his generals were well aware of the risk they had taken in throwing almost all their resources into the

Warsaw captured: Polish officers arrive at handling stations.

gamble for a quick victory in the east, and the redeployment of German divisions and higher commands from the Poland to the Westwall began before operations in Poland had even been completed. The situation faced by the British and French in October 1939 was a fait accompli. Germany had defeated Poland completely and redeployed to the Westwall forces sufficient to withstand a belated Allied offensive. Adolf Hitler's success in Poland also enhanced the Führer's opinion of his own abilities as a strategist and encouraged him to adopt the dangerous habit of discarding the advice of his military staff and senior commanders. Germany's increasing strength and the continued inactivity of the Western Allies soon inclined Hitler to order planning to commence for a fast-moving campaign to subjugate France and destroy the British Expeditionary Force. Only the onset of winter and the strongest objections from his military advisers prompted Hitler to delay his campaign until the following spring.

Lessons learned by the Wehrmacht

The German forces took advantage of the opportunity to observe the effectiveness and utility of their new weapons and other materiel, organization, and tactics in combat operations in Poland and a number of improvements were found necessary. Some changes could be made before the campaign in France the following spring, while others would have to wait.

Among the infantry weapons, the Model 1934 machine gun was found to be subject to frequent stoppages in rugged field use, particularly in muddy or dusty areas. Research on a new machine gun was accelerated, and the Model 1942 that evolved would continue to operate despite exposure to many of the conditions that hampered the use of the Model 1934 weapon. The higher rate of fire of the 1942 machine gun was to be of considerable significance in later operations.

The effort expended by Germany in the development of artillery of all types was found to be justified. According to Colonel Blumentritt, operations officer for Rundstedt, the Poles themselves testified to the effectiveness of the German artillery fire in the attack on Warsaw. The defenders had received warning of air attacks with the appearance of German aircraft and the bombing had been of limited duration. The sustained artillery fire, however, wore down the resistance of the garrison of the Polish capital.

The high velocity 88mm antiaircraft gun was found to be especially effective in engaging bunkers and prepared fortifications. The VIII Corps made reference to this of the new gun in attacking the Polish fortifications at Nikolai. According to the VIII Corps account, the gun could penetrate the walls of bunkers and buildings reinforced as strong points.

The German Mark I tanks were found to be unsatisfactory in operations, and the Mark II tanks were useful only for reconnaissance. This served to confirm the belief that these tanks were too light for operations and should be replaced by heavier types. Panzer units were henceforth equipped with a larger proportion of Mark III and Mark IV tanks. The heavier of the two, the Mark IV tank was singled out by Guderian as a highly effective weapon to be produced in quantity. The Mark II tank was utilized for a time as a reconnaissance vehicle, and eventually the Mark I and II tank chassis were utilized as gun platforms for the self-propelled gun units organized for assault operations. In general, the supply of spare parts and system of maintenance for tanks was found to be inadequate for the needs of Panzer units in combat.

The victorious Germans enter Warsaw.

The rapid and overwhelming successes and light personnel losses of the new German tank force in the Polish Campaign, as illustrated by the movements of the XIX Corps across the Polish Corridor and from East Prussia to Brzesc, convinced Hitler of the effectiveness of this new weapon. In ten days of operations the XIX Corps covered 200 miles in its drive on Brzesc. Polish reserve units still assembling in the rear areas were completely surprised and destroyed before they could organize a defence. In an action at Zabinka, east of Brzesc, elements of the XIX Corps interrupted the unloading of tanks at a rail siding and destroyed the Polish armoured unit before it could deploy and give battle. The corps' losses totalled 2,236, including 650 dead, 1,345 wounded, and 241 missing, less than four percent of Guderian's entire force. Henceforth, as in the coming French Campaign, Panzer units were to play an increasingly important part in German planning.

Organisation

Guderian recommended that battalion and regimental headquarters of Panzer units be located farther forward to direct the battle. Headquarters should be more mobile, restricted to a few armoured vehicles, and well equipped with radio communication. The XIX Corps commander also recommended better communication with the supply columns and trains of the armoured and motorized units.

The light divisions were found to have little staying power in sustained operations in Poland. These divisions already had at least one tank battalion each. The addition of a sufficient number of tanks to form a tank regiment for each division made it possible to complete the planned conversion of all four light divisions to Panzer divisions, bearing the numbers 6 through 9.

The motorized infantry divisions were found to be unwieldy in operations in Poland. To permit better control, one motorized infantry regiment was detached from each of the motorized divisions.

Equipment

Some infantry commanders complained of the awkward and heavy packs carried by the troops, recommending changes to permit the individual soldier greater freedom of action and more comfort. One commander recommended the carrying of machine gun ammunition by the ammunition carriers of gun crews in containers similar to those used by mortar crews, i.e. in a special pack carried by the individual soldier rather than in boxes carried by hand. This would permit the ammunition bearer to operate a rifle, giving the gun crew more protection and fire power. In addition a special grenade sack was recommended for the individual soldier. It was also requested that one rifleman in the infantry squad be provided with a telescopic sight to permit accurate fire on small or more distant targets.

The 57th Infantry Division prepared a report on its experiences illustrating a number of the small oversights that added to the problems of the commanders of lower units. The division was a Wave II organization composed largely of reservists who had recently completed their periods of active service. During their two years of active duty, the men had been trained on the Model 1934 machine gun. When they were mobilized for the campaign

A tank officer of the Soviet army meets with his German infantry counterparts.

in Poland, many did not know how to operate the older World War I type weapon with which some Wave II units were still equipped. Another oversight was the supply of horseshoes, made to a size common to military horses but far too small for the splayed hooves of many farm horses requisitioned at the time of mobilization.

Some fault was found with the equipment carried by assault engineers. Their heavy gear made it difficult for the engineers to carry out their assault role with the infantry. It was recommended that their equipment be so distributed that the engineers would be able to operate effectively as part of the infantry-engineer team in assault operations.

Training and tactics

The infantry tactics of the Germans were criticized by Bock, who felt that too much was sacrificed to caution. This may seem somewhat contradictory, in view of the brief period of time in which the Germans destroyed a Polish force almost as strong as their own numerically and captured a number of heavily fortified areas that the Poles defended stubbornly. Bock actually had reference to the frequent delays incurred when artillery had to be brought forward to the support of infantry units. The general felt that some artillery batteries should always be attached directly to infantry units, to give close support in an attack or movement forward. The remainder of the artillery should be sufficiently mobile to move forward to support attacking infantry with little delay. Bock expressed the opinion that the old adage "The infantry must wait for the artillery" should be changed to "The artillery may not delay the infantry."

Bock further felt that the German infantry training directives were obsolete and verbose.

The commander of the northern army group was of the opinion that these regulations should be shortened and should stress the mission and aggressive action to accomplish it. Brief and pertinent regulations would be easier to remember and would impress on the officer, noncommissioned officer, and soldier the all-important task he was to perform in combat, with minimum distraction.

Another characteristic of warfare in Eastern Europe as learned by the Germans was the considerable guerrilla activity in rear areas. As a consequence, it was recommended by a number of commanders that supply trains, workshops, and other rear installations be better equipped with weapons, particularly automatic weapons, and support personnel trained in their use.

The successful night attacks of the Poles made a considerable impression on the Germans. Although already aware of the advantage of moving by night, a device they used repeatedly, the Germans did not fully appreciate the potentialities of attacking under cover of darkness until shown by the Poles. With adequate security, these operations could cause considerable confusion when launched at the boundaries between units, as demonstrated by the Polish night attack of 12th September at the junction of the 207th Infantry Division and Brigade Eberhard lines before Gdynia.

Air support

The Luftwaffe in Poland succeeded in proving its offensive power as an attack weapon, despite the protests of some senior army commanders whose troops had been bombed in close support operations. The Luftwaffe demonstrated its capabilities in isolating the Polish front by bombing bridges and rail lines, and preventing the movement of Polish supplies and troops by bombing and strafing truck columns on the roads. The Luftwaffe also rendered material assistance to advancing German armoured columns and dive bombed Polish fortifications prior to attack by the ground forces. From this point the Luftwaffe was to have an important role as part of the German attack team.

The complete cover given ground forces by the Luftwaffe in Poland worked a disservice to the Army as far as camouflage was concerned. Despite instructions, there was little actual need for advancing units to utilize available cover and concealment at halts; for artillery to put up camouflage nets to hide guns, ammunition, and prime movers; or for command posts to limit vehicular traffic in their immediate vicinity. The Polish Air Force was unable to take advantage of this laxity on the part of many units, and the pace of the campaign made it impossible for higher commanders to take corrective action while operations were still in progress. As a consequence, a poor start in camouflage discipline was made by many units, and the lack of offensive action by the Polish Air Force made it impossible to point out examples of what might occur were the Wehrmacht to be committed against an enemy possessing an air force comparable to the Luftwaffe.

The victory parade in Poland: Guderian and Kriwoschein.

More from the same series

Most books from the 'Hitler's War Machine' series are edited and endorsed by Emmy Award winning film maker and military historian Bob Carruthers, producer of Discovery Channel's Line of Fire and Weapons of War and BBC's Both Sides of the Line. Long experience and strong editorial control gives the military history enthusiast the ability to buy with confidence.

Tiger I in Combat

Tiger I Crew Manual

Panzers at War 1939-1942

Panzers at War 1943-1945

Wolf Pack - the U boats

Poland 1939

Luftwaffe Combat Reports

Sturmgeschütze

German Artillery in Combat

Panzer Combat Reports

The Panther V in Combat

German Tank Hunters

The Afrika Korps in Combat

Panzers I & II

Panzer III

Panzer IV

For more information visit www.pen-and-sword.co.uk